The BEST VEGETABLE RECIPES from Woman's Day

The
BEST
VEGETABLE
RECIPES
from
Woman's Day

BY THE
EDITORS OF WOMAN'S DAY

Houghton Mifflin Company Boston

1980

Library of Congress Cataloging in Publication Data
Main entry under title:
The Best vegetable recipes from Woman's day.
Includes index.
1. Cookery (Vegetables)   I. Woman's day.
TX801.B43   641.6'5   80–16449
ISBN 0–395–27594–6

Printed in the United States of America

V 10 9 8 7 6 5 4 3 2 1

Contents

Introduction

ONE OF THE GREAT natural treasures of this country is its endless supply of fresh vegetables and fruit. All year long, in markets throughout the land, you can find mouth-watering displays of salad greens, broccoli, green onions, cabbage, sweet potatoes, radishes, celery, carrots, and so forth. Though some vegetables, such as asparagus, still have a distinctly brief season, in most cases the barriers of nature have fallen. So-called summer squash is for sale in January; tomatoes, green beans, and corn — while never as good as when garden fresh — are on the stands year round. When the California crop of avocados peters out, the Florida one comes in. Vegetables that were once considered exotic, such as leeks and artichokes, are now commonplace.

What is more, Americans have gone back to gardening. In the suburbs and in the cities as well as in the country, people till their own plots, harvesting at least enough for the summer, often plenty to put by for the rest of the year. New and improved varieties of the old favorites have been developed: sweeter corn, disease-resistant tomatoes, sugar-snap peas that can be eaten pod and all.

Canned and frozen vegetables have improved, too, both in quality and quantity. Frozen lima beans are almost as good as fresh limas, and while nothing can match homegrown peas, the frozen ones are not bad at all. Canned tomatoes for soups and stews are excellent. Half-a-dozen kinds of canned beans, which make quick work of bean salad and soup, are on the shelf.

An astonishing number of dried beans and legumes are also available. Pink beans or black turtle beans, which you used to have to seek out in ethnic markets, are standard fare. Bulgur is sometimes stocked right next to the wild rice in supermarkets. Health-food stores carry a mind-boggling assortment of dried beans and legumes as well as several kinds of rice and other grains. The problem is no longer where to look but what to choose.

Woman's Day has always been an advocate of vegetables, and in this book we have brought together more than 250 of the best vegetable recipes that have appeared in the magazine in recent years. The emphasis is on fresh vegetables, since they are in such abundant supply most of the year, but there is nothing wrong with using frozen or canned vegetables instead when they are more convenient or economical. The recipes in this book are precise and easy to follow. Everything is explained clearly, and where there might be some doubt or confusion, as with stir-frying or omelet and soufflé making, techniques are described in detail. Generally speaking, this is a book for the average experienced cook working in a home kitchen with the kinds of tools that are usually found there.

We also assume that the reader is a careful shopper. Shopping for vegetables is actually very easy. Your eye and your hand tell you everything you need to know. Does the lettuce look fresh, or is it wilted? Is the cauliflower clean and white, or has it started to dry up and develop spots? Are the onion tops firm, or are they soft and beginning to sprout? Do the green beans snap?

In this era without clear-cut seasons, the calendar is not always a good guide to quality. Price is often a better indication of value. Asparagus, for example, is quite reasonable when in season, exorbitant when not. The price of green peppers also reflects supply. With salad greens, it is always wise to buy by the price. With local produce, on the other hand, it often is not. Succulent, vine-ripened local tomatoes in particular can cost more at a roadside stand than they do in the supermarket, but they are worth the premium.

You'll find recipes for well over sixty different vegetables in this book. Most of them are for vegetables that are generally available in the fresh, frozen, or canned state. A few — very few — are for rare vegetables, such as chayote or fennel. There are recipes here for the hobbyist and for the cook in a hurry, for those on a tight budget and those with looser purse strings. There are recipes for the timid and for the adventurous. In other words, this book contains something for everyone.

1

JUICES
AND SOUPS

Nothing fills the house and the people in it quite like a pot of homemade soup. Whether it's a light lettuce soup with sesame croutons which merely takes the edge off the appetite or a hearty Kentucky black bean soup which is virtually a meal in the bowl, the aroma and the substance of soup do wonderful things for one's state of mind, state of health, and state of purse.

Soup actually is the ultimate convenience food. Nowadays, with a food processor to speed up the chopping and puréeing operations you can put almost any soup on the table in little more than half an hour. All you will need is some canned broth or frozen homemade stock (a recipe for which appears at the end of this chapter) and a few vegetables from the garden or market. It's cheap; it's quick; it's easy.

Nearly forty soups are collected in this chapter, one for every day of the month and then some. They are arranged by strength, from the lightest kinds of juices and cold soups (some of which need no cooking at all) to hearty soups that fill you up and send you on your way. Among the forty are creamy soups and clear soups, spring soups and fall soups. These are recipes that have come from all over the world — from Russia, France, Mexico, the Near East, the South Seas — and from the four corners of the United States. All of them are well within the talents of the everyday cook who is blessed with good taste buds and a good dose of common sense.

Juices

CUCUMBER-TOMATO COCKTAIL

1 medium cucumber
2¼ cups tomato juice, fresh or canned
2 tablespoons chopped green onions with tops
1 teaspoon Worcestershire sauce
juice of 1 lemon
2 teaspoons prepared horseradish
⅛ teaspoon hot pepper sauce
½ teaspoon salt
dash of pepper
parsley

Peel cucumber and grate into tomato juice. Add remaining ingredients, except parsley, and chill for 2 hours. Strain through coarse sieve and taste for seasoning. Serve with garnish of parsley. Makes 4 servings.

VARIATION

Fresh Tomato Juice
Seed and cut up vine-ripened garden tomatoes and put them in blender or food processor. Whirl until smooth, adding water as needed for proper consistency. Strain. Season to taste with salt and pepper.

CARROT JUICE

1½ cups sliced carrots (3 large carrots)
½ teaspoon salt
2 teaspoons lemon juice

Whirl carrots, ¾ cup water, and salt in blender or food processor until puréed. Strain through cheesecloth, pressing to extract all juice. Add lemon juice and chill. Makes about 1 cup.

Cold Soups

CHILLED CUCUMBER SOUP

This soup can be made either chunky or smooth.

    1 small container (8 ounces) yogurt
    1 cup chicken broth
    1 small cucumber, peeled, seeded, and chopped
    1 can (8 ounces) diced beets, drained (optional)
    1 small clove garlic, crushed
    ½ teaspoon salt, or to taste
    ⅛ teaspoon hot pepper sauce, or to taste
    thin unpeeled cucumber slices
    minced chives or green-onion tops

   Stir together or purée in blender or food processor all ingredients except cucumber slices and chives. Cover and chill well. Serve in chilled glasses or bowls. Garnish with cucumber slices and chives. Makes 3 or 4 servings.

VARIATIONS

For a vegetarian soup, replace chicken broth with an additional cup of yogurt.

Cucumber-Walnut Soup
   Add ½ cup chopped walnuts and omit beets and hot pepper sauce. *Do not purée.* Chill. Garnish each cup with a walnut half.

CREAM OF CUCUMBER SOUP

2 tablespoons butter or margarine
6 green onions, chopped (⅔ cup)
1 small onion, chopped
3 medium cucumbers (about 1½ pounds), peeled, seeded, and
    chopped
2 medium new potatoes, peeled and diced
2 cups chicken broth
½ cup heavy cream
1 teaspoon salt, or to taste
¼ teaspoon white pepper, or to taste
chopped radishes (optional)
minced parsley or chives

In heavy saucepan, melt butter and sauté onions until soft. Add cucumbers, potatoes, and broth; bring to boil, cover, then simmer 15 to 20 minutes, or until potatoes are tender. Cool. Whirl in blender or food processor until smooth. Chill, covered, several hours. Stir in cream, salt, and pepper. Top with radishes, if desired, and parsley or chives. Makes 4 servings.

AVOCADO-SPINACH SOUP

1 large ripe avocado, peeled, pitted, and cut up
1 cup spinach leaves, firmly packed
2 cups beef or chicken broth
milk or light cream
salt and pepper
1 lemon, cut in wedges

Whirl avocado, spinach, and broth in blender or food processor until smooth. Add enough milk or cream to make 4 cups and blend in. Season to taste with salt and pepper. Chill and taste again for seasoning. Serve with lemon wedges. Makes 4 servings.

GAZPACHO

1 loaf (1 pound) French bread
2 cloves garlic
3 tomatoes, peeled and seeded
1 large onion
1 cucumber, peeled and seeded
½ cup olive oil
¼ cup red wine vinegar, or more to taste
salt and pepper
croutons
finely diced cucumber, tomato, onion, parsley, hard-cooked egg
    for garnish

Cut up bread, soak in water, and squeeze almost dry. Put in blender or food processor with garlic and coarsely cut tomatoes, onion, and cucumber. Run machine until contents are thoroughly mixed. With machine still turned on, remove feeder cover and add oil gradually. Pour soup into bowl and stir in vinegar, salt, and pepper to taste. Chill. Put croutons and garnishes in condiment dishes to be passed at table. Serve soup in cups or large flat bowls, as desired. Makes 4 to 6 servings.

CHILLED CREAMY VEGETABLE SOUP

1 cup diced raw potato
¼ cup sliced green onion
1 cup raw peas, fresh or frozen
¼ cup sliced celery
1½ cups chicken broth
1 cup light cream
salt and pepper
chopped chives or parsley

Cook the vegetables, covered, in the broth until tender. Then purée in food processor or blender until perfectly smooth. Add cream and blend only long enough to mix well. Season to taste with salt and pepper; chill. Sprinkle with chives. Makes 4 to 6 servings.

COLD TOMATO SOUP WITH HERBS

1 cup beef or chicken broth
3 cups tomato juice
1 onion, grated
1 cup chopped celery
1 green pepper, minced
1 teaspoon salt, or more to taste
1 clove garlic
3 tablespoons lemon juice
dash of hot pepper sauce
2 tablespoons minced fresh basil, parsley, or chervil
½ cucumber, sliced
2 ripe tomatoes, peeled and sliced

Mix together broth and tomato juice and add the onion, celery, green pepper, and 1 teaspoon salt. Cut garlic in half and put toothpick through both halves, then add to mixture. Stir, cover, and refrigerate several hours or overnight. Just before serving, remove garlic and season to taste with lemon juice, hot pepper sauce, and additional salt if necessary. Add the herbs, sliced cucumber, and tomatoes and serve in chilled bowls. Makes 6 servings.

BEET SOUP

Beet soup is a refreshing summer favorite from Russia.

4 medium beets, cooked or canned, with 2 cups beet liquid
4 cups beef or chicken broth
1 medium onion, chopped
2 cloves garlic, cut in half and stuck on toothpicks
½ teaspoon salt, or more to taste
¼ teaspoon pepper
2 tablespoons vinegar, or more to taste
1 cucumber, peeled, seeded, and diced (optional)
½ cup sour cream
minced fresh dill

Pour beet liquid and meat broth into soup kettle. Grate beets through coarsest blade of grater. Stir beets, onion, garlic, salt, and pepper into broth. Cover and simmer for 20 minutes. Add vinegar and chill in refrigerator for several hours. Before serving, remove garlic, stir in cucumber, and taste for seasoning. Garnish each bowl with a dollop of sour cream and sprinkling of dill. Makes 6 servings.

Hot Soups

LETTUCE SOUP WITH SESAME CROUTONS

6 green onions or 1 small onion, minced
2 tablespoons butter or margarine
5 cups chicken broth
6 cups coarsely shredded lettuce, lightly packed
salt and pepper
sesame croutons (see recipe below)

Sauté onions in butter until tender, stirring occasionally. Stir in broth and bring to boil; add lettuce, cover, and simmer until lettuce is wilted, about 4 minutes. Season with salt and pepper. Serve with sesame croutons. Makes 6 servings.

Sesame Croutons

Heat 2 tablespoons oil in heavy skillet. Add 2 cups ½-inch white bread cubes and stir constantly over medium heat until lightly toasted and crisp, about 3 minutes. Sprinkle with 1 tablespoon sesame seed and dash of salt. Stir and toast 1 minute longer.

VARIATION

Escarole Soup

Wash and shred 1 pound escarole (1 large or 2 small heads) and add it in place of lettuce. Simmer until crisp-tender, about 10 minutes. Add about ½ cup cooked rice, if desired, for extra body; simmer for 1 or 2 minutes to warm through. Serve piping hot.

SPINACH SOUP

This simple, elegant soup is delicious hot or cold.

3 tablespoons butter or oil
1 medium onion, chopped
1 pound bulk spinach or 1 cello bag (10 ounces) spinach, washed
    and shredded
2 tablespoons flour
5 cups beef broth, hot
¼ cup heavy or sour cream, or more to taste
salt, pepper, and nutmeg
chopped parsley or chervil (optional)
croutons (optional)
grated Swiss or Parmesan cheese (optional)

Melt butter in soup kettle or large saucepan; add onion and sauté lightly. Stir in spinach and cook until it wilts. Sprinkle with flour; cook briefly. Gradually stir in hot broth and bring to boil. Reduce heat and simmer about 12 minutes. Cool slightly, stir in cream and seasonings to taste. For a cold soup, chill in refrigerator for several hours; sprinkle with herbs before serving. For a hot soup, reheat just before serving. Garnish with croutons and grated cheese, if desired. Makes 6 servings.

Note: Soup can be puréed before you add cream and seasoning.

VARIATIONS

Watercress Soup

Substitute 2 bunches watercress for spinach, setting aside several sprigs for garnish. Proceed as above. Soup may be chilled.

Sorrel Soup

Substitute ½ to 1 pound sorrel (schav) for spinach. Proceed as above. To prevent curdling, boil sweet cream before adding it to soup. Sour cream may be spooned directly from container, at room temperature. For a heartier soup, slip a poached egg into each bowl. Also excellent chilled.

Kale Soup

Remove coarse stems from 1 pound washed kale and shred leaves. Follow directions for spinach soup, using either chicken or beef broth. Garnish with hard-cooked eggs cut in half, if desired.

Cabbage Soup

Substitute 3 cups shredded cabbage plus 1 medium potato, peeled and diced, for spinach. Continue as in master recipe, puréeing soup before adding cream and seasoning. Sprinkle with chopped parsley or dill.

SPRING GREENS SOUP

about 18 medium green onions with some tops, sliced (2 cups)
2 large cloves garlic, crushed
¼ cup butter or margarine
6 cups chicken broth
2 medium new potatoes, peeled and finely diced (1½ cups)
2 small carrots, thinly sliced diagonally (½ cup)
1 pound escarole, chicory, spinach, or romaine, trimmed, washed, and cut crosswise in thin strips
½ teaspoon pepper, or to taste
¼ teaspoon salt, or to taste
½ cup heavy cream (optional)
minced parsley (optional)
grated Parmesan cheese (optional)

In Dutch oven or large kettle, sauté onions and garlic in butter until tender, stirring occasionally. Stir in broth, potatoes, and carrots. Bring to boil, cover, and simmer about 10 minutes or until vegetables are tender. Stir in greens, pepper, and salt. Bring back to boil. Cover and simmer 5 to 10 minutes, or until greens are tender. Stir in cream; heat but do not boil. Add more salt and pepper if needed. Garnish with minced parsley and grated Parmesan, if desired. Makes 6 servings.

BROCCOLI SOUP

2 tablespoons butter or margarine
1 small onion, minced
2 tablespoons flour
5 cups beef or chicken broth
1 medium head broccoli, cut up, or 2 packages (10 ounces each)
    frozen chopped broccoli
1 egg yolk
½ cup heavy or light cream
salt and pepper
nutmeg (optional)
1½ tablespoons chopped chervil, parsley, or chives
croutons (optional)

Melt butter in large saucepan. Add onion and sauté a few minutes. Sprinkle with flour, stir, and gradually add broth. Bring to boil, stirring, until thickened. Add broccoli, cover, and simmer until broccoli is tender, 10 to 15 minutes. Beat together egg yolk and cream, then add some hot soup while continuing to beat. Slowly pour egg mixture into soup, stirring constantly. Season to taste with salt and pepper, and nutmeg if desired. Reheat carefully before serving, sprinkle with chopped herbs, and garnish with croutons. Makes 6 servings.

Note: You may purée the soup before you add egg yolks, cream, and seasoning. Save a few broccoli flowerets for garnish and pass the rest of the soup through a food mill or blender. Continue as above.

VARIATION

Cauliflower Soup
Substitute 1 medium head of cauliflower, broken into flowerets, or 2 packages (10 ounces each) of frozen cauliflower for broccoli and follow directions above for plain or puréed soup. *Do not season with nutmeg.*

MUSHROOM SOUP

½ pound mushrooms
4 cups rich chicken or veal broth
2 tablespoons butter
2 tablespoons flour
½ teaspoon salt, or more to taste
dash of cracked pepper
¼ teaspoon ginger
½ cup light cream (optional)
chopped parsley

Remove stems from mushrooms and chop fine. Add to broth, bring to boil, and simmer, covered, 20 minutes. Thinly slice caps and sauté in the butter in saucepan 2 to 3 minutes. Blend in flour and seasoning. Gradually stir in stock with chopped mushroom stems and cook, stirring, until slightly thickened. Add cream, if desired, and sprinkle with parsley. Makes 4 servings.

ITALIAN GARLIC SOUP

5 cloves garlic, peeled and pressed
1 tablespoon olive oil
2 quarts rich chicken broth
salt and pepper
pinch each thyme and rosemary
2 egg yolks, beaten
½ cup light cream
thick slices Italian bread, toasted
¼ cup grated Parmesan cheese

Sauté garlic in oil until light brown. Add hot broth and seasoning. Simmer 1 hour; strain. Beat egg yolks with cream and stir a bit of broth into mixture. Then add mixture to soup. Pour over toast in tureen or individual soup bowls. Sprinkle with grated Parmesan cheese. Makes 8 servings.

Vera Cruz Garlic Soup

Make a clear soup as explained above, with either chicken or beef broth. (*Do not add egg yolks and cream.*) Place a slice of toasted Italian bread and a poached egg in each bowl, pour the soup over them, and garnish with minced parsley.

FRENCH ONION SOUP

Long considered a hangover cure in France, this soup is good anytime, anywhere.

> 1½ pounds large sweet onions
> about 5 tablespoons butter
> 4 cups beef or chicken broth
> 2 cups dry white wine, or additional stock
> salt and pepper
> ½-inch slices French bread, toasted
> 1 cup grated Gruyère cheese, or mixture of Parmesan and Emmentaler (Swiss) cheeses

Peel onions and slice thin. Melt 4 tablespoons butter in soup kettle or large saucepan. Brown onions, add stock and wine, and bring to boil. Simmer, covered, ½ hour, or until onions are tender. Season with salt and pepper to taste. Pour into large oven-proof casserole or individual earthenware tureens. Top with toast, sprinkle with cheese, and dot with remaining butter. Bake in preheated 350° oven until cheese melts, about 10 minutes. Serve with more cheese on the side. Makes 6 servings.

CLEAR TOMATO SOUP WITH YOGURT

> 4 cups tomato juice
> 2 cups chicken broth
> 2 tablespoons finely snipped parsley
> 1 teaspoon grated onion
> 1 stalk celery, minced

dash of Worcestershire sauce
1 clove garlic, crushed
½ teaspoon salt
1 teaspoon sugar
3 whole cloves
1 tablespoon lemon juice
1 egg white, beaten until frothy
6 lemon slices
6 tablespoons plain yogurt

Put tomato juice, broth, parsley, onion, celery, Worcestershire sauce, garlic, salt, sugar, and cloves in a saucepan, bring to a boil, and simmer, uncovered, about 30 minutes. Remove garlic and cloves. Add lemon juice and egg white and mix well. Taste for seasoning. Float lemon slices on top and serve with yogurt on the side. Makes 6 servings.

CORN AND TOMATO CHOWDER

2 tablespoons chopped onion or green onion
1 tablespoon chopped green pepper
¼ cup diced celery
2 medium new potatoes, peeled and diced in small pieces
3 tablespoons butter
1 can (1 pound) tomatoes, drained and chopped
1 cup corn kernels, cooked, canned, or frozen
3 cups milk, scalded
1 teaspoon salt, or more to taste
dash of pepper
1 teaspoon sugar
3 tablespoons chopped fresh dill

Cook onion, green pepper, celery, and potatoes in butter 2 or 3 minutes. Add tomatoes and cook until potatoes are done, about 10 minutes. Add corn and stir in the hot milk. Season to taste, reheat, and garnish with chopped dill. Makes 6 servings.

CORN CHOWDER, SOUTHERN STYLE

¼ pound salt pork, diced
1 small onion, chopped
2 tablespoons chopped green pepper
2 medium potatoes, diced
¾ cup diced celery
1½ cups boiling water
1 cup whole-kernel corn, cooked
½ teaspoon salt
dash of pepper
2 teaspoons flour
1 can (14½ ounces) undiluted evaporated milk

Cook pork slowly in kettle until crisp. Remove bits and pour off all but 2 tablespoons fat (reserve an additional 2 teaspoons fat). Sauté onion and pepper in fat 2 or 3 minutes. Add potatoes, celery, water, corn, salt, and pepper. Bring to boil, cover, and simmer 15 minutes, or until potatoes are done. Blend reserved pork fat with flour and stir in, along with milk. Bring back to boil, stirring, and cook until all floury taste is gone, 5 to 10 minutes. Correct seasoning, add pork bits, and serve. Makes 4 servings.

POLYNESIAN CARROT-WATERCRESS SOUP

This is a sophisticated soup with a tropical touch. Serve it to precede grilled chicken or fish.

3 tablespoons butter or margarine
3 tablespoons flour
salt
1 teaspoon curry powder
3 cups milk
1½ cups coarsely shredded carrots
1 cup chopped watercress
fresh or canned papaya, diced
chopped macadamia nuts
shredded coconut

Melt butter and blend in flour, ¾ teaspoon salt, and curry powder. Gradually add milk and cook, stirring, until thickened. Cook carrots, covered, in 1 cup water until tender. Add watercress and cook 1 minute. Add to hot milk mixture and bring to simmer. Add a little more salt if necessary. Garnish with papaya, macadamia nuts, and coconut and serve at once. Makes 6 servings.

RUTABAGA-POTATO SOUP

1 small rutabaga (about 1 pound)
1 teaspoon salt, or more to taste
3 medium potatoes, peeled and thinly sliced
2 cups milk
1 cup chicken broth
½ teaspoon sugar
dash of pepper
2 tablespoons butter or margarine

Peel rutabaga and cut in small pieces. Add 1 teaspoon salt and 1½ cups water. Cook, covered, 15 to 20 minutes. Add potatoes and cook about 10 minutes (do not drain). Purée in food mill, blender, or food processor; add milk and broth. Season to taste with additional salt, sugar, and pepper. Just before serving, reheat and stir in butter. Makes 6 servings.

LEEK-POTATO SOUP

4 medium potatoes, peeled and sliced
3 medium leeks, thinly sliced, including tender part of green tops
    (2 cups)
1 medium onion, coarsely chopped
⅓ cup butter or margarine
dash of pepper
1 teaspoon salt, or more to taste
6 cups chicken broth or water
½ cup heavy cream (optional)

In soup kettle or large saucepan, sauté potatoes, leeks, and onion in 3 tablespoons butter for 5 minutes, stirring occasionally. Add pepper, 1 teaspoon salt, and the broth or water. Bring to boil, cover, and simmer until potatoes are tender, about 20 minutes. Mash or put through food mill and correct seasoning. When ready to serve, reheat to simmer and stir in remaining butter and cream if desired. Makes 8 servings.

Note: This soup is excellent cold as well. Make a smooth purée, bind it with cream, and chill overnight. Taste for seasoning before serving.

LENTIL SOUP WITH SPINACH

    1 pound lentils, washed
    10 cups water
    2 large onions, chopped (2 cups)
    2 ribs celery, chopped (1 cup)
    2 large cloves garlic, crushed
    1 tablespoon salt, or to taste
    ½ teaspoon pepper, or to taste
    1 cello package (10 ounces) fresh spinach, stems discarded and
        leaves chopped, or 1 package (10 ounces) chopped frozen
        spinach, thawed
    juice of ½ lemon (about 1 tablespoon)

In large kettle, bring to boil lentils, water, onions, celery, garlic, salt, and pepper. Cover, then simmer about 40 minutes, or until lentils are tender, stirring occasionally. Add spinach and more salt and pepper if necessary. Cover and simmer until spinach wilts, about 10 minutes. Stir in lemon juice. Serve in warm soup bowls. Makes 8 servings.

VARIATION

You may use one pound Swiss chard in place of spinach.

BUTTERNUT SOUP

1 butternut squash (about 1 pound)
1 medium onion, quartered
1 tart apple, cored and chopped
1 strip (2-inch by 1-inch) zest of lemon
6 cups chicken broth
1 teaspoon salt, or more to taste
pepper
½ cup heavy cream
3 tablespoons sherry
paprika

Peel, seed, and cut the squash in ½-inch cubes. Put the squash, onion, apple, and lemon zest in large saucepan with broth, 1 teaspoon salt, and pepper to taste. Bring to boil, cover, and simmer until squash is tender, about 25 minutes. Discard lemon peel and purée the soup to a fairly smooth consistency. Correct seasoning. Just before serving, stir in the cream and sherry and simmer soup for 10 minutes. Sprinkle with paprika and serve. Makes 6 servings.

VEGETABLE SOUP

Use whatever is fresh in the market or garden to make this soup your very own creation.

3 tablespoons oil
3 cups chopped vegetables (mixture of onion, carrot, celery, kohlrabi or turnip or rutabaga, leeks or green onions)
1 cup green beans, cut in spoon-sized pieces
6 cups stock or water
1 can (1 pound) tomatoes, cut up, with juice
⅓ cup rice
1 can (1 pound) kidney or pinto beans
1 pound escarole, spinach, or Savoy cabbage, rinsed and shredded
1 cup sliced mushrooms
salt and pepper
3 tablespoons minced parsley

Heat oil in soup kettle and sauté chopped vegetables for 10 minutes. Stir in green beans, broth, and tomatoes, and simmer, covered, 20 minutes. Add rice and continue simmering until vegetables are nearly tender, about 20 minutes more. Add canned beans, greens, and mushrooms and cook until greens are tender, 5 to 10 minutes. Season to taste with salt and pepper, garnish with parsley, and serve. Makes 8 to 10 servings.

VARIATION

Two potatoes, diced, or ½ cup macaroni may be used instead of rice. Other fresh vegetables, such as peas, zucchini, or broccoli, may be added with or in place of the green beans.

YANKEE BEAN SOUP

Save the bone from baked ham to make a soup that's really a main dish.

    1 pound dried pea beans or other small white beans
    3 medium onions, chopped
    2 carrots, diced
    2 bay leaves
    4 cloves garlic (optional)
    3 or 4 celery tops
    few sprigs parsley
    1 ham bone with some meat
    salt and pepper
    1 to 2 tablespoons vinegar, to taste

Following directions on page 129, soak the beans either overnight or by the short-soak method. Add onions, carrots, bay leaves, garlic if desired, celery tops, parsley, and ham bone. Bring to boil and simmer, covered, about 1½ hours, or until beans are barely tender. Add hot water if soup gets too thick. Discard bay leaves, garlic, celery, and parsley. Remove meat from bone and put morsels back in soup. Season to taste with salt, pepper, and vinegar.

Mash 1 cup of beans to thicken soup, if desired. Reheat before serving. Makes 10 servings.

Note: If ham bone is not available, use any smoked pork bone.

TAMPA ESCAROLE SOUP

 1 cup (about ½ pound) dried pea beans, rinsed and picked over
 2 tablespoons oil
 3 medium onions, chopped
 1 large green pepper, chopped
 2 large cloves garlic, crushed
 1 meaty ham bone
 4 medium potatoes, diced
 1 head escarole, sliced
 1 teaspoon salt, or more to taste
 ¼ teaspoon pepper, or to taste
 1 to 2 tablespoons vinegar
 hot pepper sauce

Soak the beans as explained on page 129. Heat oil in skillet over medium-high heat and sauté onions, green pepper, and garlic until lightly browned; stir into beans. Add ham bone and bring to boil. Reduce heat, cover, and simmer 1¼ hours, or until beans are nearly tender, adding hot water if soup gets too thick. Remove bone; cut off any meat and add it to soup. Add potatoes and escarole and cook 15 minutes, or until potatoes are tender. Season to taste with salt, pepper, and vinegar. Season with hot pepper sauce, if desired, at the table. Makes 8 servings.

VARIATION

For a vegetarian soup, omit ham bone and add ¼ cup oil.

KENTUCKY BLACK BEAN SOUP

2½ cups (1 pound) dried black beans
1 cup chopped onions
¼ cup oil
4 whole cloves
4 allspice berries or ⅛ teaspoon ground allspice
6 peppercorns or ⅛ teaspoon ground pepper
¼ teaspoon nutmeg
salt
juice of ½ lemon (1 to 1½ tablespoons)
⅓ cup sherry (optional)
2 tablespoons butter or margarine
lemon slices

Soak the beans as directed on page 129. Add onions, oil, and spices (with whole cloves, allspice, and pepper wrapped in cheese-cloth). Bring to boil, reduce heat, and simmer 45 minutes, or until beans are tender, adding more hot water as necessary. Discard spices and purée soup. Season to taste with salt and lemon juice. Stir in sherry and butter and reheat. Garnish with lemon slices. Makes 8 servings.

Note: Be careful not to overcook; black beans sometimes cook faster than other types of dried beans.

STOCK

Make and freeze your own stock to use as a base for sauces and soup and in pilaf or risotto. Regard the following recipe as a guide, adding vegetables you have on hand as well as trimmings and left-over vegetables and bones.

3 pounds veal or beef bones, preferably with marrow, or chicken
     backs and giblets
2 onions
2 carrots
2 ribs celery with leafy tops
2 leeks (if available)

2 sprigs parsley
1 bay leaf
2 cloves garlic
¼ teaspoon peppercorns
1 tablespoon salt, or more to taste

Put bones or chicken parts in a very large pot and add water to cover. Bring to boil and simmer, skimming froth. Add the vegetables, with parsley, bay leaf, garlic, and peppercorns tied together in a piece of cheesecloth, and 1 tablespoon salt. Skimming fat from time to time, simmer, covered, for a least 2 hours for chicken, 3 hours for veal or beef. Strain and discard soup vegetables, herbs, and bones, saving the marrow to spread on toast and the chicken meat for another dish. Skim thoroughly and taste for seasoning. Refrigerate or freeze in handy containers. (Refrigerated stock should be boiled every 4 days to keep it from spoiling.) Makes about 2 quarts.

Note: You may also make broth without bones.

2

HOT AND COLD SANDWICHES

It used to be that a sandwich was a sandwich was a sandwich, but not anymore. Two slices of white, whole wheat, or rye bread enclosing a slice or two of processed meat or cheese or a scoop of tuna salad — the standby of Mother's kitchen and the downtown lunch counter — just isn't good enough anymore.

The big bread explosion of the 1970s revolutionized the sandwich. In addition to the traditional loaf, we now have grainy bread, crusty French baguettes, pita (sandwich pockets), rolls, long loaves, round loaves, and square loaves to choose from on the supermarket shelf. And those skillful people who make their own bread can — and do — go on and on *ad infinitum*, experimenting with grains, shapes, and flavorings.

What good bread needs, however, is a filling that does it proud. Thin slices of leftover roast piled high with watercress and sliced radishes, spears of asparagus or broccoli grilled and served piping hot, falafel (spicy chickpea balls) — all these make sandwiches that are a meal in themselves. Open sandwiches such as the French pizza, pissaladière, can be cut to snack, lunch, or canapé size.

Additional sandwich and filling ideas appear elsewhere in this book, under appetizers (chili and cheese slices), main dishes (Oriental chicken salad), and so on. In looking for new fillings, be guided by the principle that if you can eat it from a plate, you can eat it on a slice of bread.

BROILED ASPARAGUS SANDWICH

¼ cup crumbled blue cheese (about 1 ounce)
4 ounces whipped cream cheese
2 tablespoons milk
1 tablespoon minced onion
4 slices white, cracked wheat, or oatmeal bread, toasted
butter or margarine
1 to 1½ pounds fresh asparagus, or 2 packages (10 ounces each)
    frozen asparagus spears, cooked and well drained

In small bowl, blend well cheeses, milk, and onion. Spread bread lightly with butter; arrange 4 or 5 asparagus spears on each slice, and top with a generous dollop of cheese mixture, spreading slightly. Broil 6 inches from heat 2 minutes, or until bubbly. Serve at once. Makes 4 servings.

Note: If you have a food processor, save a few pennies by whipping a 3-ounce package of regular cream cheese yourself. Then blend in the blue cheese, milk, and onion and proceed with the recipe.

MUSHROOM-CHEESE SANDWICH

1 pound mushrooms, chopped
2 tablespoons butter or margarine
1 cup shredded Cheddar cheese
1 egg, slightly beaten
8 slices bread
2 medium tomatoes, sliced

Sauté mushrooms in the butter about 5 minutes. Remove from heat. Add cheese and egg and mix well. Toast bread on one side. (Thin slices of French bread, cut on the bias, are ideal. If French bread is not on hand, use white or cracked wheat bread.) Spread mushroom mixture on untoasted side. Top with tomato slice and put under broiler 5 to 8 minutes, or until heated. Makes 4 servings.

BAKED BROCCOLI AND CHICKEN SANDWICH

1 loaf (7 or 8 ounces) Italian or French bread
mayonnaise
¾ pound cooked chicken or turkey, sliced
salt and pepper
¾ pound fresh or 1 package (10 ounces) frozen broccoli, cut in
    3-inch pieces, cooked until crisp-tender, and well drained
⅔ cup coarsely shredded natural Swiss cheese, packed
2 tablespoons chicken broth or milk

Split bread lengthwise and place cut side up on cookie sheet. Cut each in half; spread with mayonnaise. Arrange chicken or turkey on bread and season to taste with salt and pepper. Top with broccoli. Stir together ½ cup mayonnaise, cheese, and broth or milk until well blended. Spoon or spread over broccoli. Bake in preheated 425° oven until bubbly and golden brown, about 10 minutes. Makes 4 servings.

PISSALADIÈRE

The French have their own version of pizza, though it's hard to say where one lets off and the other begins.

pizza base (see note)
olive oil
2 cans (15 or 16 ounces each) Italian-style tomatoes
¼ cup tomato paste
2 tablespoons butter or margarine
2 large sweet onions, quartered, then sliced (about 4 cups)
½ cup grated Parmesan cheese
oregano
1 can (2 ounces) anchovy fillets
oil-cured black olives, pitted

Prepare pizza base and set aside. In saucepan, combine 2 tablespoons oil, tomatoes, and tomato paste and cook, uncovered, stirring occasionally, 45 minutes, or until thick. Melt butter in skillet, add onions, and sauté until soft and golden. To assemble, brush dough with oil and sprinkle with cheese, top with onions, then sprinkle with oregano to taste. Cover with tomato mixture. Arrange anchovies in lattice effect on top and put an olive in center of each square. Brush olives with oil and bake in preheated 400° oven 25 minutes, or until crust is thoroughly baked. Brush with oil before serving. Makes 4 servings.

Note: Use your favorite homemade or frozen pizza dough or pie dough. Roll out a large round pizza, individual 6-inch pizzas, or a large rectangular pizza to cut in squares.

FALAFEL IN PITA

Tiny fried chickpea balls in pita — this sandwich is a spicy treat from the Middle East.

> 2 cups chickpeas, canned or home-cooked, drained
> 2 slices whole wheat bread, day-old or lightly toasted, crumbled
>   fine (about ⅔ cup)
> ½ cup onion, chopped
> 1 egg
> 2 tablespoons minced parsley
> 3 cloves garlic, minced
> tahini sauce (see recipe below)
> ½ teaspoon salt
> ½ teaspoon each turmeric and baking soda
> ¼ teaspoon each cumin, marjoram, basil, and pepper
> oil
> 4 large pita breads or 8 small ones, heated and cut in half
> shredded lettuce
> chopped tomato
> chopped cucumber

In large bowl, mash chickpeas. Add bread, onion, egg, parsley, garlic, 1 tablespoon tahini sauce, the salt, turmeric, baking soda, cumin, marjoram, basil, and pepper; mix well. With wet hands, shape in 24 balls. Heat ½ inch oil in skillet (or use deep-fryer) to 350° and fry the balls, a few at a time, until well browned. Drain on paper towels. Put 3 balls into each pita half, top with lettuce, tomato, and cucumber, and sprinkle with tahini sauce. Makes 8 servings.

Tahini Sauce

In screw-top jar, combine 1 cup sesame oil, ¼ cup cold water, juice of 3 lemons, 2 tablespoons minced parsley, 1 crushed clove garlic, and ½ teaspoon salt. Store in refrigerator. Shake before using. Makes 1½ cups.

CHALUPA

3 cups refried beans, homemade or canned
¼ cup beer, or more if needed
oil
12 corn tortillas, packaged or fresh (4 to 6 inches in diameter)
½ head lettuce, shredded
2 or 3 medium tomatoes, chopped
4 ounces Monterey jack cheese, shredded (1 cup)
taco or Mexican-style hot sauce

Slowly heat the refried beans, then stir in enough beer to bring them to the consistency of soft mashed potatoes. Meanwhile, heat ¼ inch oil in skillet and fry tortillas quickly one at a time until crisp, about 4 seconds per side, making sure each tortilla is immersed in oil. Add oil as needed. Drain on paper towels. Spread about ¼ cup hot bean mixture on each tortilla. Add lettuce, tomatoes, and cheese. Spoon on hot sauce to taste. Makes 6 servings.

ONION-CUCUMBER SANDWICH

12 thin slices white or whole wheat bread
whipped butter or margarine
1 medium cucumber, peeled
1 medium onion, peeled
salt and pepper

Spread bread lightly with butter. Slice cucumber and onion in very thin slices. Arrange cucumber in overlapping rows on 6 of the bread slices, covering bread completely but keeping layer thin. Top with thin, overlapping layer of onion. Sprinkle lightly with salt and pepper. Cover with remaining bread slices. Press firmly together and cut on diagonal. Makes 6 servings.

OPEN ROAST BEEF AND RADISH SANDWICH

This is a wonderful way to dress up that leftover roast.

> 6 slices rye bread
> whipped butter or Dijon mustard
> ½ pound roast beef, thinly sliced
> salt and pepper
> watercress
> about 6 red radishes, thinly sliced

Spread bread with butter or mustard and divide beef evenly. Season with salt and pepper and cut in half. Arrange watercress and radishes on top; salt radishes if desired. Makes 6 servings.

VARIATION

This sandwich is excellent when made with cold lamb instead of roast beef.

SARDINE AND CUCUMBER SANDWICH

> 2 cans (3¾ ounces each) sardines, drained
> 3 tablespoons minced watercress or parsley
> 3 tablespoons mayonnaise
> 1 tablespoon grated onion
> 1 teaspoon lemon juice, or to taste
> 8 slices pumpernickel or other dark bread
> 1 small cucumber, peeled and thinly sliced

In medium bowl, mash sardines. Stir in watercress or parsley, mayonnaise, onion, and lemon juice. Spread sardine mixture on 4 slices of bread; add cucumber slices. Top with remaining bread. Makes 4 servings.

PAN BAGNA

From the Riviera, this is a sandwich with the kiss of Mediterranean sunshine.

> 2 loaves (7 or 8 ounces each) French or Italian bread
> ¼ cup olive oil
> 1 clove garlic, split
> 1 large tomato, thinly sliced
> 1 large green pepper, cut in strips
> ½ cup oil-cured black olives, pitted
> 1 medium red onion, sliced
> ½ can (2 ounces) flat anchovies, drained
> red wine vinegar
> pepper

Cut each loaf in two and then in half lengthwise; remove a little bread from each piece to form a shallow hollow. Brush with olive oil, then rub with garlic. Layer bottoms with some tomato slices, green pepper, olives, onion, and anchovies. Sprinkle with vinegar and season with pepper to taste. Cover with bread tops, pressing down with hands. Wrap each airtight. Weight down with heavy object 30 minutes. Remove weight; refrigerate until ready to serve. Makes 4 servings.

Note: Other ingredients may be added to the sandwich, if desired: for example, canned tuna (drained and flaked), ratatouille, or cold chicken.

3

APPETIZERS
AND
SIDE DISHES

In the world of vegetables, *appetizer* and *side dish* are very elastic terms; depending on when and how it is served, almost any vegetable dish can act as one or the other. A small helping of salad might open a meal instead of close it, certain meatless main dishes might be stretched out to serve as side dishes, and so on. What we have done in the chapter that follows, then, is to offer only a few hot and cold appetizers, ones that are ideal for both stand-up and sit-down parties, for guests and family alike. The appetizers are followed by conventional side dishes, which are grouped by cooking method: fried, boiled or steamed, braised, and baked. Three grain pilafs are included for good measure.

Here is something for every taste: spicy or bland, sweet or sharp, fresh or smoky. The choice of vegetables ranges from such familiar favorites as corn, potatoes, asparagus, and tomatoes to some of the more exotic vegetables, such as fennel and salsify. There is at least one recipe for each season and for every occasion, from the humblest to the most exalted.

In many of the recipes, two or more vegetables are combined, often in unexpected ways. Limas and leeks, for example, or sesame cauliflower and peppers ought to shake the mothballs out of anyone's culinary imagination. A few unusual fruit and vegetable combinations are also on hand, among them a novel way to prepare beets with orange juice (orange-ginger beets) and a new twist for sweet potatoes, sweet potatoes with apricot sauce.

With very few exceptions, the appetizers and side dishes presented in this chapter are easy to prepare. A food processor is a big help with eggplant caviar and hummus, both of which used to be beaten by hand for hours, but for the most part the only special equipment you will ever need is a cutting board and a sharp knife.

Appetizers

EGGPLANT CAVIAR

A delicate, smoky dip, eggplant caviar is to be found in every land within the old Fertile Crescent. Season your caviar as much or as little as you like, but do serve it at room temperature to allow all the subtleties of flavor to emerge.

> about 2 pounds eggplant, preferably small
> ¼ cup lemon juice, or more to taste
> 2 or 3 cloves garlic
> ½ cup olive oil
> ¼ cup tahini (sesame seed paste; see note)
> salt
> ¼ cup minced parsley (preferably the flat Italian kind)

If possible, grill the eggplants over charcoal on a well-oiled grill, turning frequently, until tender, 45 minutes to 1 hour. Otherwise, wrap them in aluminum foil and bake in a preheated 375° oven until tender, about 30 to 45 minutes. Scrape out the pulp, getting as close to the skin as possible, and if it appears watery, squeeze out the liquid. Put the pulp in a blender or food processor with the lemon juice and garlic and process until fairly smooth. Add the oil and tahini, whirling until you have a pale, smooth cream. Taste for seasoning. Just before serving, heap the eggplant caviar on a plate, make a border of parsley, and arrange dipping vegetables around it. Makes about 2 cups.

Note: Tahini can be purchased at any Middle Eastern food store as well as in most specialty food shops and health-food stores.

HUMMUS

Hummus is a rich, smooth dip or spread originally from the southern and eastern shores of the Mediterranean. Try it with pita bread, whole wheat crackers, or vegetables, such as zucchini or green peppers, sliced for dipping.

  ½ cup lemon juice, or more to taste
  1 or 2 cloves garlic
  1 can (15 or 16 ounces) chickpeas, drained
  about ¾ cup tahini (sesame seed paste)
  salt
  oil-cured black olives
  paprika
  olive oil (optional)

Put the lemon juice and garlic in a blender or food processor and start whirling. Add the chickpeas a handful at a time. Shake up or stir the tahini and add gradually. If the mixture gets too thick and hard, add a spoonful of water. Continue whirling until smooth and creamy. Taste for seasoning, adding more lemon juice or salt if needed. When ready to serve, mound the hummus on a plate, surround it with olives, sprinkle with paprika, and dribble with olive oil if desired. Makes about 1½ cups.

Note: One cup (about ½ pound) dried chickpeas or garbanzos may be used instead of the canned ones; see soaking and cooking directions on page 129.

MUSHROOMS WITH ALMOND-BREAD STUFFING

  1 pound large mushrooms, with wide caps
  lemon juice
  salt and pepper
  ¼ cup butter or margarine
  ⅓ cup sliced or slivered almonds
  1½ cups fine soft bread crumbs
  ¼ cup minced parsley

Remove stems from mushrooms and chop. Put caps in greased shallow baking dish and sprinkle lightly with lemon juice, salt, and pepper. Melt butter in small skillet. Add stems, almonds, and crumbs and sauté, stirring, 3 to 4 minutes. Stir in parsley and divide evenly among mushroom caps. Bake in preheated 375° oven 15 to 20 minutes, or until filling is crisp and caps are tender. Makes about 12.

GUACAMOLE

    1 clove garlic, halved
    2 ripe avocados
    3 tablespoons lime or lemon juice
    1 hot chili pepper, chopped, or ¼ teaspoon hot pepper sauce
    1 tablespoon grated onion
    salt

Rub bowl with garlic halves, then mash avocado pulp with fork in same bowl. Add juice, chili pepper or hot pepper sauce, grated onion, and salt. Chill until serving time. Makes about 1½ cups.

CHILI AND CHEESE SLICES

    1 loaf (7 or 8 ounces) French or Italian bread, sliced ½ to ¾
        inch thick
    ½ cup butter or margarine, softened
    1 can (4 ounces) jalapeño or other green chilies, drained and
        finely chopped
    ¼ cup green olives, pitted and minced
    1 small clove garlic, minced
    4 ounces shredded Cheddar cheese (1 cup)

Toast bread on one side under broiler; set aside. Blend well butter, chilies, olives, and garlic; spread on untoasted side of bread. Sprinkle cheese on top. Broil 7 inches from heat source until bubbly and lightly browned, about 10 minutes. Serve immediately. Makes 6 servings.

Note: When they are available, use fresh hot chilies. Remove seeds and ribs under running cold water and chop the flesh. Wash your hands with soap and water immediately after handling the chilies. Do not touch your eyes or face before washing your hands.

STUFFED ARTICHOKES

4 large artichokes
½ lemon
1½ cups dry bread crumbs
½ cup grated Romano cheese
2 tablespoons chopped parsley
1 cup water
4 tablespoons oil, divided

Cut off artichoke stems and discard small outer leaves. With kitchen shears, trim spiny tips from remaining leaves. Rub cut parts of artichoke with lemon to prevent darkening. Mix crumbs, cheese, and parsley. Starting at base of each artichoke, push leaves back gently and fill with about ½ cup crumb mixture. Gently tap bottom of artichoke on hard surface to settle crumbs and distribute evenly. Pour water into large heavy saucepan. Add artichokes stem down. Sprinkle each with about 1 tablespoon oil. Cover and cook over moderate heat 45 to 50 minutes, or until leaf can easily be removed and fork pierces base easily. Add more water if necessary. Makes 4 servings.

Side Dishes

POMMES DE TERRE LORETTE

These delicate potato fritters are as light as a puff of air. The secret is the *pâte à choux* base.

½ cup butter or margarine
salt
1 cup flour
4 eggs
1 pound potatoes, peeled and cooked
pepper
nutmeg
oil or fat for deep-frying

In medium saucepan, heat 1 cup water, the butter, and ¼ teaspoon salt to boiling. Dump in flour all at once and stir over heat until dough forms a ball and leaves sides of pan. Remove from heat and beat in eggs one at a time. (This is the *pâte à choux*, which may also be made in a food processor.) Mash potatoes or force through ricer. Season with salt, pepper, and a little freshly grated nutmeg. Mix with *pâte à choux*. Heat oil to 370° on frying thermometer, or until a 1-inch square of bread browns in 60 seconds. Shape mixture into small balls on floured board; drop into hot fat and fry until golden and puffed to about double original size. Drain on paper towels and serve hot. If necessary, puffs can be reheated on a cookie sheet in a preheated 425° oven for 5 minutes. Makes about 12 servings.

POTATO PANCAKES

Potato pancakes are a Middle European specialty, good with pot roast or on their own. Garnish with sour cream or applesauce.

>   2 large baking potatoes or 3 or 4 medium potatoes (about 1 pound)
>   1 tablespoon grated onion
>   1 teaspoon salt
>   dash of pepper
>   2 tablespoons flour, matzoh meal, or cracker crumbs
>   2 eggs, well beaten
>   oil

Peel potatoes and soak 2 hours in cold water. Dry and grate medium coarse. (A blender or food processor may be used, but the product will be quite different.) Drain and press firmly to squeeze out all liquid, then add remaining ingredients, except oil. Heat ¼ inch oil in skillet to near smoking point. Drop in spoonfuls of mixture, spreading with back of spoon to diameter of 4 to 5 inches to keep cakes thin and crisp. Fry until golden brown and crisp on both sides. Serve at once. Makes 4 servings as a main dish, 6 as a side dish.

Note: For crisp, light texture and delicate flavor, follow these five rules: Use only russet (baking) potatoes. After peeling them, soak them in cold water 2 hours before grating. Use a minimum of flour or crumbs. Use plenty of oil for frying, heated to near smoking temperature. Serve pancakes while crisp and hot.

PUMPKIN PANCAKES

>   1 can (1 pound) pumpkin
>   1 cup all-purpose flour
>   1 teaspoon each salt and baking powder
>   ⅛ teaspoon pepper
>   ½ teaspoon dry mustard
>   1 egg, slightly beaten
>   2 tablespoons milk
>   oil

Mix all ingredients except oil. Drop by tablespoonfuls into ½ inch hot oil in skillet. Cook until browned on both sides and done. Serve at once. Makes 4 servings.

ZUCCHINI PANCAKES

2 medium zucchini, grated
1 teaspoon salt
1 carrot, grated
2 tablespoons minced onion
2 tablespoons minced parsley
1 egg, beaten
½ cup flour
dash of pepper
oil

In colander, mix zucchini and salt; let drain about 15 minutes, squeezing out excess liquid with back of spoon. Mix well-drained zucchini (about 1 cup), carrot, onion, parsley, egg, flour, and pepper. Drop by tablespoonfuls into ½ inch hot oil in skillet and fry until brown on both sides. Drain on absorbent paper. Serve hot. Makes 4 servings.

FRIED OKRA

2 eggs
1 tablespoon milk
½ teaspoon salt
⅛ teaspoon pepper, or to taste
1 pound okra, stems trimmed, then cut in ½-inch slices (about 4
    cups)
1 cup cornmeal
oil

In bowl, beat eggs, milk, salt, and pepper. Add okra and toss until well coated. With slotted spoon, transfer to bowl containing cornmeal. Toss until slices are well coated. In skillet, heat ½ inch oil until hot. Stir in okra and sauté until it is tender and the corn-meal is golden brown and crisp, about 10 minutes. Remove okra with slotted spoon and drain well on paper towels. Serve at once. Makes 4 servings.

FRIED ONIONS AND CORN

This is delicious with hamburgers and frankfurters.

    2 tablespoons butter or margarine
    2 tablespoons oil
    3 large onions, sliced (3 cups)
    1 medium green pepper, cut in 1-inch strips (1 cup)
    1 large clove garlic, crushed
    1 large tomato, peeled and chopped, or 1 can (8 ounces) toma-
        toes, drained and cut up
    2 teaspoons chili powder
    ¼ teaspoon salt
    ⅛ teaspoon pepper, or to taste
    about 1½ cups kernels cut from 3 ears corn, or 1 can (12 ounces)
        vacuum-packed corn
    ½ cup thinly sliced pimiento-stuffed olives

Heat butter and oil in heavy skillet; sauté onions, green pepper, and garlic until onions are almost tender, about 10 minutes, stir-ring often. Stir in tomato, chili powder, salt, and pepper. Cover and simmer until onions are tender, 10 to 15 minutes, stirring oc-casionally. Add corn and olives. Cook and stir until hot. Makes 4 servings.

CABBAGE AMANDINE

    ¼ cup butter or margarine
    ⅓ cup slivered blanched almonds
    4 cups finely shredded cabbage
    1 to 2 tablespoons lemon juice
    ½ teaspoon sugar
    salt

Heat butter in large skillet; add almonds and sauté, stirring, until golden. Remove with slotted spoon and set aside. Add cabbage, cover, and sauté 5 minutes, or until cabbage is crisp-tender. Add lemon juice, sugar, and salt to taste. Fold in almonds and heat gently. Makes 4 servings.

HOME-FRIED SWEET POTATOES

4 medium sweet potatoes
¼ cup butter or margarine
salt

Cook and peel potatoes and slice about ¼-inch thick. Melt butter in skillet and add potato slices, turning to brown evenly. Sprinkle with salt. Makes 4 servings.

Note: Cold potatoes give better results than warm ones.

VARIATION

Home-Fried New Potatoes
Use cooked and cooled new white or red potatoes, together with minced onion or scallions. Follow directions for sweet potatoes.

FRENCH-FRIED SQUASH SLICES

1 large butternut squash
fat for deep-frying
salt and pepper

Peel squash, cut in half lengthwise, and remove seeds and stringy portion. Cut in ¼-inch slices. Drop small amount at a time into deep hot fat (385° on frying thermometer) and fry 4 minutes, or until medium brown and tender. Drain on paper towels. Remove to platter and sprinkle with salt and pepper to taste. Keep warm in oven. Makes 4 servings.

VARIATION

Slices of sweet potato or strips of zucchini (salted first to draw out some of the juice) also take well to French-frying. Follow directions above.

DJUVECS

A Balkan vegetable potpourri, djuvecs is good hot or cold.

> 1 medium eggplant (about 1 pound)
> salt
> 2 medium onions, thinly sliced
> 2 large cloves garlic, crushed
> ¼ cup oil (see note)
> 2 medium tomatoes, peeled and diced
> 1 medium green pepper, seeded and cut in strips
> 1 small yellow summer squash, cut in 1½-inch strips
> 1 medium potato, diced in ¼-inch pieces
> 1 cup chicken broth or water
> ½ teaspoon pepper

Peel eggplant and dice in ½-inch pieces; sprinkle with salt and set aside for at least 20 minutes. In flameproof casserole, sauté onions and garlic in hot oil until tender, 5 to 7 minutes. Wipe eggplant dry and add it, turning until coated with oil. Stir in tomatoes, green pepper, squash, potato, broth or water, ½ teaspoon salt, and pepper. Bring to boil. Cover and simmer, stirring occasionally, 20 to 25 minutes, or until vegetables are tender and liquid has been absorbed. (Casserole may also be baked in 350° oven for about 45 minutes.) Let stand 15 minutes or more before serving. Serve warm or at room temperature. Makes 6 servings.

Note: Traditionally, djuvecs is made with olive oil if it is to be served at room temperature, ordinary vegetable oil if it is to be served hot. Cold djuvecs may need additional salt. Other seasonal vegetables — green beans, for example — may be added with or substituted for the summer squash.

ASPARAGUS WITH HOLLANDAISE

One of spring's great joys is fresh asparagus. It is good hot or cold, naked or veiled in butter or sauce.

> **2 pounds asparagus**
> **salt**
> **hollandaise sauce (see recipe below)**

Break off tough ends of asparagus. If desired, remove tough skin as well as scales from lower part of stalks with vegetable peeler. In large skillet, bring to boil 1 inch salted water. Add asparagus; bring back to boil. Boil, uncovered, 5 minutes. Cover, then simmer 5 to 7 minutes, or until barely tender. With tongs or two forks, remove to serving dish. Serve with hollandaise sauce. Makes 4 servings.

Hollandaise

> **½ cup butter**
> **yolks of 3 large eggs**
> **1 to 1½ tablespoons lemon juice, or to taste**
> **⅛ teaspoon salt**
> **dash of cayenne, white pepper, or hot pepper sauce**
> **2 tablespoons hot water**
> **minced parsley (optional)**

Heat butter in heavy saucepan until hot and foaming but not browned. In small bowl, beat egg yolks, lemon juice, salt, and cayenne with rotary beater or wire whisk, ½ minute or until very well blended. Gradually beat in butter, then water. Return to saucepan and beat over very low heat until mixture thickens slightly. Serve at once or let stand over warm water up to 30 minutes. Just before serving, sprinkle with parsley, if desired. Makes about ⅔ cup.

Blender Hollandaise

Heat butter until hot and foaming but not browned. Rinse blender container with hot water and set in place. Whirl only 2 egg yolks and 1 tablespoon water in blender with lemon juice, salt, and cayenne for 3 seconds. Remove center insert in lid and, with blender running, very slowly pour in foaming butter, except for milky residue in bottom of pan. When thoroughly blended and slightly thickened, sauce is ready to serve (do not overblend). Makes about ⅔ cup.

Note: If sauce curdles or separates, remove from heat or stop blender and beat in 1 tablespoon hot water.

BOILED CORN

Garden-fresh corn needs no more than a quick hot bath to bring it to perfection. Here is the *Woman's Day* way to boil corn.

> **8 ears corn, husks and silk removed**
> **butter or margarine**
> **salt and pepper**

Bring large kettle of water to boil. Add corn, cover, and bring to full boil. Remove from heat. Let stand covered 5 to 10 minutes or until kernel explodes when pierced with knife point. Serve with butter, salt, and pepper to taste. Makes 4 servings.

POTATOES JACQUES

> **12 small new potatoes in jackets**
> **1 small onion, minced**
> **1 clove garlic, minced**
> **1 tablespoon butter or margarine**
> **1 large carrot, peeled and finely shredded**
> **¾ cup finely diced celery (2 ribs)**
> **2¼ cups beef or chicken stock**
> **½ teaspoon salt**
> **¼ teaspoon marjoram**
> **chopped parsley**

Scrub potatoes. Sauté onion and garlic in butter or margarine in heavy saucepan, until tender but not browned. Add potatoes, carrot, celery, stock, salt, and marjoram. Bring to boil, cover, and simmer 20 to 25 minutes, or until potatoes are tender. Remove the potatoes to hot serving dish. Boil the sauce 2 minutes to reduce, then pour over the potatoes and sprinkle with parsley. Makes 6 servings.

LEMONY BRUSSELS SPROUTS AND POTATOES

1 pint fresh Brussels sprouts
4 medium potatoes, peeled and cut in 1-inch cubes
salt
2 tablespoons butter or margarine
2 tablespoons flour
1 cup milk or light cream
1 teaspoon grated lemon peel
¼ teaspoon nutmeg, or to taste

Rinse sprouts and pick off tough outer leaves. Steam sprouts and potatoes in 1 inch boiling salted water 15 minutes, or until tender; drain. Meanwhile, melt butter in saucepan and stir in flour and ½ teaspoon salt until smooth. Gradually stir in milk or cream; cook and stir over medium heat until thick and smooth. Blend in lemon peel and nutmeg. Taste for seasoning. Combine cream sauce, sprouts, and potatoes. Serve at once. Makes 4 servings.

SWEET-AND-SOUR POTATOES

⅓ cup butter or margarine
1 onion, thinly sliced
2 pounds potatoes, peeled and quartered
1 package (12 ounces) pitted prunes
1 teaspoon salt
1 tablespoon lemon juice, or more to taste
¼ cup honey

In skillet, melt butter or margarine and add onion. Sauté until golden brown. Add potatoes, brown slightly, then add prunes, salt, and 1 cup water. Cover and simmer 45 minutes. Add lemon juice and honey and stir. Taste the sauce: it should be pleasantly sweet-and-sour. Cover and simmer, stirring as needed and adding a little more water if necessary, until potatoes are tender, about 15 minutes. Makes 8 servings.

ASPARAGUS SYRIAN STYLE

1 onion, thinly sliced
¼ cup olive oil
salt and pepper
2 pounds asparagus
chopped parsley
lemon wedges

Sauté onion in oil in large skillet until tender but not browned. Add ⅓ cup hot water and salt and pepper to taste. Wash and trim asparagus and lay in skillet. Cook, covered, until tender. Remove asparagus to hot serving dish, sprinkle with parsley, and serve with lemon wedges. Makes 4 servings.

ARTICHOKE QUARTERS

4 medium artichokes
1 teaspoon salt
1 tablespoon lemon juice

In large kettle or Dutch oven, bring 2 to 3 inches water to boil. Meanwhile, cut off stems of artichokes and discard small outer leaves. With kitchen shears, trim spiny tips from remaining leaves. If desired, cut off about 1 inch from top of artichokes. (To help prevent darkening as artichokes are trimmed, rub them with the cut side of a lemon or dip them in cold water mixed with a little lemon juice or vinegar.) Cut in quarters. Add salt, lemon juice, and artichokes to boiling water. Bring back to boil. Cover and boil gently, turning occasionally, 10 to 15 minutes, or until leaf can easily be removed and base is easily pierced by fork. With slotted spoon, lift out and drain. With tip of teaspoon, remove chokes (fuzzy centers). Serve hot with melted butter, or cold with vinaigrette. Makes 4 servings.

Note: To cook artichokes whole, stand them in a saucepan and add 4 cups boiling salted water and 2 tablespoons lemon juice. Cover and boil gently 35 to 45 minutes, or until base can be pierced easily with fork. Serve as above.

SALSIFY (OYSTER PLANT)

Salsify is called oyster plant not because it looks like an oyster — actually, it resembles a skinny, dark-skinned parsnip — but because it supposedly tastes like one.

> 1 bunch salsify (about 1 pound)
> 2 tablespoons lemon juice
> salt and pepper
> butter

Cut off and discard tops of salsify; scrape roots, and to prevent darkening, drop vegetable at once into quart of water to which lemon juice has been added. Leave in water 10 minutes, then cut in 1-inch lengths and drop in boiling salted water. Cook until tender, about 10 minutes; drain and season to taste with salt, pepper, and butter. Makes 4 servings.

KOHLRABI IN CHILI SAUCE

> 4 kohlrabi
> salt
> 3 tablespoons butter or margarine, melted
> 1 tablespoon lemon juice
> 1 to 2 tablespoons chili sauce

Remove leaves from kohlrabi; peel and cut in ⅛-inch slices. Cook in lightly salted water 8 to 10 minutes, or until crisp-tender; drain. Combine remaining ingredients in saucepan and heat gently. Add kohlrabi and toss. Makes 4 servings.

Note: If desired, chop tender leaves very fine. Simmer a few minutes in boiling water, drain, and mix with sliced kohlrabi.

STEAMED GREEN ONIONS WITH EGG-BUTTER SAUCE

4 bunches small green onions (about 28)
salt
3 tablespoons butter or margarine
1 tablespoon lemon juice, or to taste
1 hard-cooked egg, chopped
pepper

Trim onions to about 8 inches; reserve tops to use for stock. Discard any tough outer leaves. In ½ inch boiling, lightly salted water in skillet, steam onions, covered, until crisp-tender, about 3 minutes. Drain well and turn into heated serving dish. Melt butter in skillet, add lemon juice and egg, and taste for salt. Stir and heat through. Pour over onions and season with pepper. Makes 4 servings.

BRAISED GREENS

2 pounds greens (see note)
¼ cup oil, preferably olive
1 small onion, thinly sliced (¼ cup)
1 large clove garlic, crushed
1 teaspoon salt
pepper
vinegar or lemon juice

Wash the greens thoroughly. Shake off the excess water. Cut leaves crosswise in three or four pieces, discarding tough stems and yellowing leaves. Heat oil in Dutch oven or kettle, sauté onion slices and garlic 2 to 3 minutes, stirring often. Add greens, tossing just until wilted. Cover and braise until tender, 10 to 15 minutes. Season with salt and pepper. Add vinegar or lemon juice to taste. Turn into warm serving dish. Makes 4 servings.

Note: Just about any kind of greens can be cooked this way: escarole, Swiss chard, tender turnip or mustard greens, beet tops, rappini (*broccoli di rape*), collards, or kale.

RED CABBAGE

¼ cup goose fat, butter, margarine, or oil, heated
1 large onion, chopped
1 large head red cabbage, shredded (about 4 pounds)
2 large tart apples, cored, peeled, and coarsely chopped
⅓ cup red wine vinegar, or to taste
2 teaspoons each salt and sugar, or to taste
¼ teaspoon each ground allspice and cloves, or to taste
¼ cup red currant jelly (optional)
minced parsley

Combine all ingredients except jelly and parsley in large kettle or Dutch oven. Cover and simmer 1 hour, or until cabbage is wilted and flavors are well blended, stirring occasionally. Stir in jelly, if desired, and taste for seasoning. Sprinkle with parsley. Makes 10 to 12 servings.

BRAISED CELERY AND TOMATOES

1 tablespoon butter or margarine
2 cups celery, cut in 1-inch pieces
½ teaspoon salt
⅛ teaspoon pepper
1 teaspoon sugar (optional)
1 can (1 pound) tomatoes
chopped parsley

Melt butter, add celery, and sauté a few minutes. Season with salt, pepper, and sugar if desired. Drain tomatoes and add juice to celery. Cover and simmer 10 minutes, or until tender. Add tomatoes, cut in quarters or halves, and heat. Sprinkle with a little parsley. Makes 6 servings.

FENNEL PARMIGIANA

4 heads fennel
salt and pepper
½ cup butter or margarine, melted
¾ cup grated Parmesan cheese

Trim green tops and tough outer stalks from fennel. Trim base and slice fennel from top to bottom in ¼-inch slices. Cook in boiling water about 5 minutes, or until tender. Drain and season with salt and pepper to taste. Place half the fennel slices in buttered shallow baking dish. Pour on half the melted butter and sprinkle with half the cheese. Top with remaining fennel, butter, and cheese. Bake in preheated 425° oven about 10 minutes. Makes 4 servings.

GERMAN-STYLE BRAISED CUCUMBERS

3 slices bacon
3 medium cucumbers, peeled, seeded, and cut in ¼-inch slices
2 tablespoons vinegar
½ teaspoon salt
¼ teaspoon pepper, or to taste
minced radishes (optional)

Cook bacon in large skillet until crisp. Drain on paper towels, crumble, and set aside. Drain off all but 2 tablespoons fat. Add cucumbers; fry over medium-high heat 5 minutes, or until slices are well coated with fat. Reduce heat and stir in bacon, vinegar, salt, and pepper. Cover and simmer until cucumbers are crisp-tender, about 5 minutes, stirring occasionally. Garnish with radishes, if desired. Makes 4 servings.

PLAKI

Plaki is green beans with an Armenian touch.

> ½ cup water
> salt
> 1 pound green beans (preferably the flat Italian kind), trimmed and cut diagonally in 1½-inch pieces
> 1 large onion, thinly sliced
> 1 large clove garlic, crushed
> 3 tablespoons oil, preferably olive
> 2 medium tomatoes, peeled and diced
> ½ cup minced parsley, plus some for garnish
> ½ teaspoon pepper
> 5 thin slices lemon, quartered
> additional lemon slices (optional)

Parboil beans in boiling salted water, drain, and set aside. In a saucepan, sauté onion and garlic in oil until tender, 5 to 7 minutes. Stir in green beans, tomatoes, ½ cup parsley, pepper, and ¼ teaspoon salt. Bring to boil. Cover and simmer, stirring occasionally, about 15 minutes, or until beans are crisp-tender. Add quartered lemon slices. Serve hot, cold, or at room temperature. Garnish with additional parsley and lemon slices, if desired. Makes 4 servings.

DILLED BRUSSELS SPROUTS

> 1 pint fresh Brussels sprouts, or 1 package (10 ounces) frozen sprouts
> salt
> ½ cup yogurt
> 2 tablespoons snipped fresh dill, or 1 teaspoon dried dill weed

Cook fresh sprouts in boiling salted water until crisp-tender, about 10 minutes, and drain. (Follow package directions for frozen sprouts.) Beat yogurt lightly with a fork, stir in the dill, and pour over sprouts. Makes 4 servings.

SESAME CAULIFLOWER AND PEPPERS

1 tablespoon sesame seed
2 tablespoons oil
1 clove garlic
1 small head cauliflower, broken into flowerets
1 small green pepper, seeded and sliced
¾ teaspoon salt
⅛ teaspoon hot pepper sauce

In heavy saucepan, stir sesame seed over medium heat until lightly toasted, about 5 minutes; remove from pan. Add oil and garlic and cook until garlic is browned; discard garlic. Add cauliflower and green pepper; stir to coat with oil. Add water, salt, and hot pepper sauce; cover and cook until flowerets are crisp-tender, about 8 minutes. Uncover and cook a few minutes longer, until liquid evaporates. Toss with sesame seed and serve immediately. Makes 6 servings.

JERUSALEM ARTICHOKES WITH TOMATOES

The Jerusalem artichoke is a tuber that looks like a small, knobby potato or celery root. It has a very elusive flavor. Jerusalem artichokes are sometimes marketed as "sunchokes."

1 pound Jerusalem artichokes
salt
2 tablespoons butter or margarine
2 tablespoons olive oil
1 cup canned tomatoes
pepper
1½ teaspoons minced fresh basil, or ½ teaspoon dried basil

Cook the Jerusalem artichokes in boiling salted water until tender, 10 to 15 minutes. Drain and rub off skins; slice. Heat butter and oil. Add tomatoes, salt and pepper to taste, and basil. Cook over low heat, stirring constantly, until tomatoes melt into sauce. Add artichoke slices and reheat until hot. Makes 4 servings.

LIMAS AND LEEKS

2 packages (10 ounces each) frozen lima beans
2 leeks, thinly sliced
2 tablespoons butter or margarine
1 tablespoon flour
¼ teaspoon paprika
salt and pepper

Cook lima beans according to package directions; drain, reserving ½ cup liquid. Cook leeks in butter for 5 minutes; sprinkle with flour and paprika and cook 1 minute more. Blend in bean liquid and simmer, stirring constantly, until thickened. Season to taste with salt and pepper, add beans, and reheat. Makes 6 servings.

STEWED CORN MEDLEY

3 medium onions, thinly sliced
3 tablespoons butter or margarine
3 green peppers, sliced
3 tomatoes, cut up
2 cups cut fresh corn
salt and pepper

Cook onion in melted butter 2 or 3 minutes. Add peppers and tomatoes. Bring to boil, then simmer, covered, 10 minutes. Add corn and simmer, covered, 5 minutes, or until corn is tender. Season to taste. Makes 6 servings.

ORANGE-GINGER BEETS

1 pound beets
½ teaspoon grated orange peel
¾ cup orange juice
1 tablespoon cornstarch
2 teaspoons sugar

½ teaspoon ginger
⅛ teaspoon salt
1 tablespoon butter or margarine

Place beets in saucepan, cover with boiling water, cover, and cook until tender, 45 to 60 minutes. Cool under cold running water, cut off tops, and slip off skins. Cut in julienne strips; set aside. In small bowl, mix well orange peel and juice, cornstarch, sugar, ginger, and salt. Melt butter in medium skillet. Add beets and orange-juice mixture; stir over medium heat until sauce boils. Boil 1 minute. Makes 4 servings.

Note: Canned beets may substitute for fresh ones. Drain a 1-pound can of julienned beets and proceed to make the sauce.

HONEYED PARSNIPS

3 medium parsnips (about 1 pound)
salt
2 tablespoons butter or margarine
1 tablespoon honey
1 teaspoon grated orange rind
2 tablespoons orange juice

Peel parsnips and cut in ¼-inch diagonal slices. Cook in small amount of lightly salted boiling water until tender, about 15 minutes. Drain, add remaining ingredients, and simmer a few minutes. Makes 4 servings.

BERMUDAS GLACES

6 Bermuda onions
2 tablespoons butter
¼ cup honey
½ teaspoon paprika
½ teaspoon salt
dash of pepper

Halve the onions and put them cut side up in a large buttered casserole. Mix the honey, paprika, salt, and pepper with 3 tablespoons water and spread over onions. Dot with butter, cover and bake in preheated 350° oven for 1½ hours, basting occasionally. Makes 6 servings.

BRAISED ESCAROLE AND TOMATOES
WITH CANNELLINI

> 2 cloves garlic, crushed
> 2 tablespoons oil, preferably olive oil
> 1 can (16 ounces) tomatoes, cut up
> ½ teaspoon salt, or more to taste
> 1 hot pepper, or dash of hot pepper sauce
> 1 pound escarole (1 large or 2 small heads), rinsed well and
>   drained
> 1 can (16 ounces) cannellini (white kidney beans) rinsed and
>   drained

In saucepan large enough to hold all the escarole, sauté garlic in hot oil until lightly browned. Add tomatoes, salt, hot pepper, and escarole. Cover and steam 10 to 12 minutes, stirring occasionally. Add beans for last 5 minutes of cooking time. Makes 4 servings as a main dish, 8 as a side dish.

OVEN ASPARAGUS

> 2 pounds asparagus
> 2 tablespoons butter or margarine
> ½ teaspoon salt

Wash and trim asparagus and put in two-quart casserole. Dot with butter and sprinkle with salt. Cover and bake in preheated 350° oven about 45 minutes. Makes 4 servings.

TOMATOES STUFFED WITH TOMATOES

These make an elegant — and amusing — garnish for roast lamb.

> 4 large tomatoes
> salt and pepper
> 1½ tablespoons minced fresh basil or dill
> 1 basket cherry tomatoes (at least 24)
> olive oil

Cut tomatoes in half and scoop out some of the pulp; reserve for another dish. Season shells with salt, pepper, and herbs and fill with cherry tomatoes. Drizzle with olive oil. Bake in preheated 450° oven for 10 minutes. Serve immediately. Makes 8 servings.

BAKED TOMATOES WITH CORN PUDDING

> 6 large tomatoes
> salt
> 1 egg, separated
> 1 teaspoon sugar
> 3 tablespoons butter
> 1½ cups corn pulp (see note)

Cut tops off tomatoes and scoop out pulp; reserve for other use. Sprinkle with salt and turn upside down to drain while preparing pudding. Stir egg yolk, sugar, ½ teaspoon salt and 1 tablespoon melted butter into corn pulp. Fold in stiffly beaten egg white. Fill tomatoes with the mixture and set in buttered shallow baking dish. Dot with butter. Bake in preheated 350° oven 45 minutes, or until pudding is puffed and golden-brown. Makes 6 servings.

Note: To prepare corn pulp, take a sharp knife and slit down center of each row of kernels on an ear of corn. Push out pulp and juice with dull edge of knife. Allow 6 ears of corn for 1 cup of pulp.

VARIATION

Green Peppers with Corn Pudding

Take 6 medium-large green peppers, core, and parboil 5 minutes in boiling salted water. Drain and cool. Fill with corn pudding and proceed as for tomatoes.

BROILED TOMATOES

> 4 ripe tomatoes
> salt
> 2 teaspoons chopped fresh or ½ teaspoon dried basil
> ¼ cup minced onion
> fine dry bread crumbs
> butter or margarine

Cut tomatoes in half and put on baking sheet. Salt them and sprinkle with basil and onion. Top each with about 1 teaspoon of crumbs and dot with butter. Broil until heated and lightly browned on top; if you prefer, bake tomatoes in 425° oven about 10 minutes. Makes 4 servings.

GRILLED CHERRY TOMATOES

> 1 basket (about 24) cherry tomatoes
> salt
> olive oil

Wash and stem cherry tomatoes and put them in a fireproof dish or skillet. Sprinkle with salt and drizzle with olive oil. About 5 minutes before serving, place pan on grill; keep shaking so that tomatoes roll around and cook evenly. Serve immediately. Makes 4 to 5 servings.

Note: Instead of using the grill, you can put cherry tomatoes in an ovenproof dish and bake in a preheated 425° oven for 5 to 10 minutes. Be careful not to overcook.

ROASTED PEPPERS

Slightly fussy to prepare, roasted peppers are well worth the effort.

  6 large green peppers
  ⅓ cup olive oil
  ¼ cup minced parsley
  ½ teaspoon pepper
  ½ teaspoon salt
  2 large cloves garlic, crushed

Spear stem end of pepper with long fork and roast over high gas flame, or broil, until skin is black and blistered, about 5 minutes, turning peppers as they roast. Peel and scrape off skin with sharp knife. Remove core and seeds. Do not rinse. Cut in slices and combine with remaining ingredients. Chill. Toss before serving. Makes 6 servings.

BAKED GREEN PEPPERS AND ONIONS

  2 cups each sliced green peppers and onions
  2 tablespoons butter or oil
  salt and pepper

Put all ingredients in 1½-quart casserole. Cover and bake in 350° oven about 45 minutes. Makes 4 servings.

BROILED EGGPLANT SLICES

  salt
  2 eggplants (about 1 pound each), peeled and cut in ½-inch
    slices
  ½ cup oil, preferably olive oil
  ½ to ¾ teaspoon pepper
  2 large cloves garlic, crushed
  parsley sprigs

Sprinkle salt on both sides of eggplant slices. Let stand 20 to 30 minutes, then rinse under cold water and dry on paper towels. Combine oil, pepper, ¼ teaspoon salt, and garlic. Place eggplant on broiler rack. Brush with oil mixture. Broil 4 inches from heat about 10 minutes, or until golden brown, brushing occasionally with oil mixture and turning once. Garnish with parsley. Makes 4 servings.

INDIVIDUAL BAKED EGGPLANT PACKETS

1 eggplant (about 1 to 1½ pounds), peeled and cut in 8 wedges
salt
1 large tomato, cut in 8 wedges
1 large onion, thinly sliced
4 teaspoons olive oil
½ teaspoon pepper
½ teaspoon basil
4 small cloves garlic, crushed

Salt eggplant and set aside for 20 minutes; wipe dry and proceed. For each serving, place on square of foil 2 wedges each eggplant and tomato, ¼ of onion slices, 1 teaspoon olive oil, ⅛ teaspoon each pepper and basil, 1 clove garlic, and dash of salt. Fold edges of foil over vegetables and crimp to seal well. Place packets on baking sheet and bake in preheated 375° oven, turning occasionally, 30 minutes, or until eggplant is tender. Makes 4 servings.

BROILED MUSHROOMS

1½ pounds large mushrooms
butter or vegetable oil
salt and pepper
hot toast points (optional)

Break off mushroom stems and reserve for other use. Wipe caps with damp paper towel. With fingers, butter or oil each cap well. Arrange round side up in shallow pan and put under broiler unit about 5 inches from source of heat. Broil 4 to 5 minutes, then turn and broil on other side 4 to 5 minutes. Sprinkle with salt and pepper to taste and, if desired, serve on hot toast points. Makes 4 servings.

CORN COOKED IN ROASTING WRAP

8 ears corn, husks and silk removed
½ teaspoon sugar (optional)
butter or margarine
salt and pepper

Place 4 ears corn in center of large piece of roasting wrap or in roasting bag. Add 3 tablespoons water. Sprinkle with ¼ teaspoon sugar, if desired. Seal wrap as directed on package. Repeat with remaining ears. Place in shallow baking pan. Cook in preheated 400° oven 20 to 25 minutes, or until kernel explodes when pierced with knife point. Serve with butter, salt, and pepper to taste. Makes 4 servings.

GRILLED CORN

8 ears corn
water
butter or margarine
salt and pepper

Pull back husks from corn; remove silk. Replace husks and if necessary tie in place. Soak in cold water 15 to 30 minutes. Broil 4 to 6 inches from heat in broiler or over hot coals, turning occasionally, about 20 minutes or until kernel explodes when pierced with knife point. Serve with butter, salt, and pepper to taste. Makes 4 servings.

Note: Husked corn may be soaked, then wrapped in foil and grilled.

GRATIN DAUPHINOIS

This is the most famous dish from Dauphiné, a beautiful region in southeastern France. Some chefs say the potatoes must be baked slowly in cream only; others say to add cheese; still others add eggs to that. Each is perfection.

> butter
> 6 medium potatoes sliced wafer thin
> salt and black pepper
> nutmeg
> about 2 cups light cream (not half-and-half)

Butter a baking dish no deeper than 2 inches. Layer three-quarters full with potatoes, salt, pepper, and a little nutmeg. Pour in cream just to top of potatoes. Dot with 2 tablespoons butter. Bake in preheated 250° oven for 1½ hours, or until potatoes are tender, most of cream absorbed, and top browned. Makes 6 servings.

SWEET POTATOES WITH APRICOT SAUCE

> ¼ cup butter or margarine
> 1 cup brown sugar, firmly packed
> 1 cup apricot nectar
> 2 teaspoons grated lemon rind
> ¼ teaspoon cinnamon
> dash of nutmeg
> 4 or 5 medium sweet potatoes, cooked, peeled, and cut in 1-inch
>   slices
> pecan halves (optional)

Melt butter in saucepan and add sugar, nectar, lemon rind, and spices; heat to boiling and boil gently just a few minutes. Arrange potatoes in 12 x 8 x 2-inch baking dish, pour sauce over them, sprinkle with pecans, if desired, and bake in preheated 350° oven 30 minutes, or until potatoes are heated through and sauce is bubbly. Makes 8 servings.

BAKED GRAPEFRUIT AND SWEET POTATOES

2 grapefruit
½ cup brown sugar, packed
½ teaspoon salt
¼ teaspoon cinnamon
1½ pounds (4 to 6) sweet potatoes, cooked or canned
2 tablespoons butter or margarine

Peel and section grapefruit, working over bowl to reserve juice. Combine reserved juice, sugar, salt, and cinnamon. Arrange potatoes and grapefruit in shallow 1½-quart baking dish. Pour syrup mixture over potatoes and dot with butter. Bake in preheated 350° oven 30 minutes. Makes 4 servings.

ACORN SQUASH STUFFED WITH CREAMED SPINACH

This dish is as pleasing to the eye as it is to the palate.

2 acorn squash
2 tablespoons butter or margarine, melted
salt, pepper, and nutmeg
1 package (10 ounces) frozen creamed spinach, thawed
chopped toasted almonds (optional)

Place squash in roasting pan with 1 inch water and bake in preheated 400° oven 30 minutes. Remove from water and let cool 10 minutes (save water in pan). Cut in half lengthwise and scoop out seeds. Return to pan, cut side up; brush with butter, season with salt, pepper, and nutmeg to taste, and fill with spinach. Cover with foil and bake 30 minutes, or until tender. Sprinkle with almonds, if desired. Makes 4 servings.

Note: You may use about 2 cups homemade creamed spinach instead of frozen creamed spinach.

RATATOUILLE

Ratatouille is a delightful summer medley from the south of France.

> oil, preferably olive oil
> 3 cloves garlic, crushed
> 2 large onions, sliced
> 2 small eggplants, cubed
> 4 small zucchini, sliced
> 2 green peppers, cut in strips
> 1 head fennel, sliced (optional)
> 1 can (1 pound) tomatoes, preferably plum tomatoes
> 1 tablespoon chopped fresh basil, or 1 teaspoon dried basil
> 1½ teaspoons salt
> 1 teaspoon chopped parsley
> pepper

Heat about ⅓ cup oil in heavy skillet and add garlic and onions. Cook until wilted. Add eggplants, zucchini, peppers, and fennel if desired, tossing until all are coated with oil. (It may be necessary to add more oil.) Stir in the tomatoes, basil, salt, parsley, and pepper to taste; cover and simmer, stirring occasionally, for 1 hour. Uncover and cook down until most of liquid has evaporated and mixture is thick. Taste for seasoning. Serve hot or cold. Makes 6 servings.

ZUCCHINI CASSEROLE

> 1 pound zucchini
> salt
> 3 tablespoons oil
> ¼ pound mushrooms, sliced
> 3 scallions, minced
> 1 clove garlic, minced
> 1½ teaspoons chopped fresh basil, or ½ teaspoon dried basil
> pepper
> 2 medium tomatoes, sliced
> 4 ounces mozzarella cheese, sliced

Slice zucchini ¼-inch thick, sprinkle with salt, and set aside for 20 minutes. Squeeze out and pat dry. Heat oil in skillet and sauté zucchini until golden; remove to 1½-quart casserole. Sauté mushrooms in oil, adding more if necessary; add scallions and cook 2 minutes, then add garlic and cook 1 minute more. Spread mixture over zucchini, sprinkle with the basil and salt and pepper to taste. Arrange tomato slices on top, then cover with cheese. Bake in preheated 375° oven until brown and bubbly, about 30 minutes. Makes 4 servings.

SPINACH AND BROCCOLI AU GRATIN

> 2 pounds fresh spinach or 2 cello packages (10 ounces each) spinach
> 3 tablespoons butter or margarine
> 3 tablespoons flour
> salt
> 1½ cups milk
> 1 small head broccoli or 1 package (10 ounces) frozen chopped broccoli, cooked and drained
> pepper
> nutmeg
> ½ cup grated Parmesan cheese

Rinse spinach in cold water, remove tough stems, tear leaves in small pieces, and drain. With only the water that clings to the leaves, steam spinach in large covered kettle over medium heat 10 to 15 minutes, or until tender, stirring often; drain. Meanwhile, melt butter in small saucepan and stir in flour and 1 teaspoon salt until smooth. Gradually blend in milk and cook, stirring constantly, until smooth and thick. Combine spinach and broccoli and season with salt, pepper, and nutmeg to taste. Mix in cream sauce and ⅓ cup Parmesan cheese and turn into greased 10 x 6 x 2-inch glass baking dish. Sprinkle with remaining cheese and bake in preheated 350° oven 25 minutes, or until bubbly and lightly browned. Makes 6 servings.

BAKED BREADED BROCCOLI SPEARS
WITH CHEESE SAUCE

6 tablespoons butter or margarine
1 cup fine dry bread crumbs
salt and pepper
2 eggs
1¼ cups milk
1½ pounds broccoli, parboiled, or 2 packages (10 ounces each)
     frozen broccoli spears, thawed and drained
2 tablespoons flour
dash of cayenne
¼ pound Cheddar cheese, shredded (1 cup)

Melt 4 tablespoons butter in saucepan. Stir in crumbs and ¼ teaspoon each salt and pepper; set aside. Lightly beat eggs with ¼ cup milk. Dip or brush spears lightly with egg mixture, then coat with crumb mixture. Place on lightly greased cookie sheet and bake in preheated 425° oven 25 to 30 minutes, or until spears are tender and crumbs browned. Meanwhile, melt remaining 2 tablespoons butter in saucepan. Stir in flour, ¼ teaspoon salt, and the cayenne; cook and stir until bubbly. Gradually stir in remaining 1 cup milk; cook and stir until mixture thickens and begins to boil. Cook 1 minute longer. Add cheese; stir until melted. Taste for seasoning and serve with broccoli. Makes 4 servings.

VEGETABLE MEDLEY

2 carrots, peeled and cut in small chunks
¼ pound green beans, cut up
1 box (10 ounces) frozen baby lima beans
salt
1 small yellow summer squash, sliced
4 green onions, sliced
2 tablespoons butter or margarine
pepper

Put the carrots, green beans, and limas with ½ teaspoon salt in a saucepan and pour on enough boiling water barely to cover. Simmer, covered, for 10 minutes, then add squash and onions. Cover and cook until vegetables are tender, about 10 minutes. Drain and add the butter and salt and pepper to taste. Makes 4 servings.

GREEN PEA AND BARLEY PILAF

1 onion, thinly sliced
3 tablespoons oil
1 cup hulled whole barley
3 cups vegetable, beef, or chicken broth, heated
1½ cups green peas, fresh or frozen
salt and pepper

In 2½-quart flameproof casserole or small Dutch oven, sauté onion in oil until soft. Stir in barley; cook until lightly browned. Add broth; heat to boiling. Cover and bake in preheated 350° oven 35 to 40 minutes, or until barley is almost tender. Stir in peas. Cover; bake 10 minutes, or until barley and peas are tender, adding more hot broth or water if mixture is too dry. Season to taste with salt and pepper. Makes 4 to 6 servings.

BULGUR-NUT PILAF

1 cup bulgur (cracked wheat; see note)
3 tablespoons butter or oil
2 cups beef or chicken broth
2 medium carrots, shredded
½ teaspoon salt
½ cup chopped walnuts, pecans, or almonds

In 2½-quart flameproof casserole, sauté bulgur in butter or oil about 5 minutes to brown lightly, stirring occasionally. Stir in broth, carrots, and salt; bring to boil. Cover and bake in preheated

350° oven, stirring occasionally, 25 minutes, or until broth is absorbed. Stir in nuts. Makes 4 servings.

Note: Bulgur is available in health-food stores, in specialty food shops, and on the ethnic or gourmet foods shelf of supermarkets.

VARIATION

Mushroom and Bean Sprout Pilaf

When sautéing bulgur, add ¼ pound sliced mushrooms. Omit carrots; continue as above. After 20 minutes, stir in 1½ cups bean sprouts and ½ large green pepper, chopped. Cover and cook 5 minutes longer. Omit nuts. If desired, serve with soy sauce. Makes 4 servings.

LENTIL-STUFFED GREEN PEPPERS

    1 cup lentils
    salt
    2 teaspoons vinegar, or to taste
    4 tablespoons butter or margarine
    1 onion, chopped
    4 tablespoons grated Parmesan cheese
    pepper
    4 or 5 medium green peppers
    ½ cup fine soft bread crumbs
    1 can (8 ounces) tomato sauce

Put lentils in saucepan and add 2½ cups water. Bring to boil, cover, and simmer 35 minutes, or until liquid is absorbed and lentils are tender. Season to taste with salt and vinegar. In small skillet, melt 2 tablespoons butter or margarine; add onion and sauté until golden. Add to lentils. Add 2 tablespoons cheese and season with salt and pepper to taste. Split peppers in half lengthwise, core, and parboil in boiling salted water about 5 minutes. Drain and fill with lentil mixture. Brown crumbs lightly in the remaining butter and sprinkle, with remaining cheese, on peppers. Set peppers in shallow baking dish and surround with sauce. Bake in preheated 350° oven about 30 minutes. Makes 4 or 5 servings.

4

SALADS

I t is hard indeed to imagine life without salads. Great bowls of leafy greens, colorful marinated vegetables, shimmering molded salads, slews of slaws — hardly a day goes by without a salad of one kind or another on the table in many homes.

We are fortunate in this country to be able to buy salad fixings all year round. Greens of some kind are always available, and when one kind looks wilted or is too expensive, another is always right there to take its place. Tomatoes, okra, cucumbers, green peppers, and avocados have their seasons, but other fresh vegetables, such as celery, green beans, carrots, mushrooms, green onions, and zucchini, as well as dried beans, grace our markets virtually all year long. Cabbage, too, is ever present, be it green or new cabbage, Chinese cabbage, red cabbage, or the beautiful and mellow Savoy cabbage.

Woman's Day has long been an advocate of salads: the fifty or so recipes in this chapter were culled from the hundreds and hundreds that have appeared in the magazine over the years. They run the gamut from an old-fashioned German cabbage salad to up-to-the minute ideas, such as sprouts with yogurt dressing. There are economical salads (caraway cabbage slaw) and extravagant ones (Belgian endive and mushroom salad). In other words, there is a salad here for every taste, including the least adventurous and the most daring.

SALAD TIPS

• For contrast in mixed green salads, pick a mixture of light and dark greens and a balance of textures. Always be guided by appearance and price when making your choice. No one can afford to buy wilted or overpriced produce.

• A large variety of lettuce and other greens is available year round, including Bibb, Boston, romaine, and iceberg lettuce, chicory, escarole, and leaf lettuce, spinach, watercress, and Belgian endive. All kinds of cabbage — green, white, Savoy, red, Chinese — are also available. Exotic greens, such as bok choy and arugula, are carried in ethnic markets and specialty shops.

• To prepare greens for salads, wash them thoroughly, changing the water until it rinses clean. Have the final water very cold. Shake off any excess and spin the greens in a plastic salad spinner. If you do not have one, use a wire salad basket or blot the greens dry with paper towels or a clean kitchen towel. Put the greens in a plastic bag or container and store them in the refrigerator.

• Before serving a salad, chill the serving bowl and individual salad plates. Tear the greens with your fingers.

• Coat fruits that darken after being cut (avocados, apples, pears), as well as mushrooms, with dressing or lemon juice as soon as you cut them. Mix others with dressing just before serving.

• Fresh herbs add immeasurably to a salad. Parsley, chives, and mint, among the more familiar ones, are always good; chervil, basil, or tarragon gives any salad a special lift.

• Sprouts, such as alfalfa and mung bean sprouts, are a delicious and nutritious addition to a salad. Sesame seeds and nuts (chopped walnuts, slivered almonds, pine nuts, and so on) also provide added crunch — and protein.

• Salad dressings serve three functions: they contribute to and bring out flavor, they bind the ingredients, and they add food value. In most cases, you should add dressing just before serving. Be sparing rather than generous: much of a salad's appeal lies in its crispness. Recipes for vinaigrette, mayonnaise, and green sauce follow; other sauces are worked into individual salad recipes.

Dressings

VINAIGRETTE

The classic vinaigrette, made with either vinegar or lemon juice and oil, drops a thin veil of sauce over salad greens, altering nature in slight but significant ways. Find the ratio of vinegar to oil that pleases you (the recipe that follows is only a guide), using top-quality ingredients for best results. Try adding fresh herbs — chives, chervil, basil, tarragon, or parsley — to vary the sauce on occasion. In other words, write your own recipe!

> 1 tablespoon wine vinegar or lemon juice, or more to taste
> ½ teaspoon Dijon mustard (optional)
> salt and pepper
> ¼ cup olive oil or salad oil, or a mixture of both

With a fork, beat vinegar or lemon juice, mustard, and a pinch of salt and pepper in the bottom of a salad bowl. Beat in oil little by little until well blended. Taste for seasoning. Makes about ¼ cup, or enough to coat about 4 cups of torn salad greens.

Note: You may make a larger quantity of dressing in a screw-top jar and store it in the refrigerator for several days. Shake well before using.

MAYONNAISE

Homemade mayonnaise is one of those foods that linger on in memory long after they have passed the palate. Learn to whip up your own — it is remarkably easy with a mixer or food processor — and make your salads truly memorable.

2 egg yolks
salt
½ teaspoon dry mustard
lemon juice
2 cups olive oil or salad oil, or a mixture of both
white pepper

Beat egg yolks with a fork, rotary beater, whisk, or electric mixer until they are creamy. Beat in ½ teaspoon salt, mustard, and 2 teaspoons lemon juice. Very gradually add oil, beating until thickened. Thin with lemon juice if necessary. Season to taste with pepper and additional salt and lemon juice. Store tightly covered in the refrigerator for up to one week. Makes about 2 cups.

VARIATION

Food Processor Mayonnaise
Add one whole egg to the egg yolks; whirl them together with the salt, mustard, and lemon juice for 1 minute. Proceed as above, gradually adding the oil with the machine running. Stop from time to time to check consistency; add more lemon juice if needed. Correct seasonings.

GREEN SAUCE

A mayonnaise offspring, green sauce is superb with cold fish or chicken and summer vegetables, notably tomatoes and cucumbers.

½ cup coarsely chopped watercress (including stems), or tender spinach leaves
½ cup coarsely chopped parsley
1 bunch (about 6) green onions, coarsely chopped
⅔ cup mayonnaise
⅓ cup sour cream
salt and pepper
1 teaspoon lemon juice

Whirl the watercress, parsley, and green onions together with the mayonnaise and sour cream in a food processor or blender.

Season to taste with salt, pepper, and lemon juice. Keeps well in refrigerator for two weeks. Makes about 1½ cups.

VARIATION

Parsley-Dill Sauce
You can make a similar dressing by using 1 cup parsley and 2 tablespoons chopped fresh dill in place of the watercress-parsley-green onions combination.

Green Salads

TOSSED GREEN SALAD WITH MUSHROOMS AND RED ONIONS

½ pound mushrooms, sliced
3 tablespoons lemon juice
½ cup plus 1 tablespoon salad oil
1 red onion, sliced and separated
4 cups torn spinach leaves
4 cups torn salad greens (Boston, romaine, or other lettuce)
salt and pepper

Marinate mushrooms in combined lemon juice and oil. Just before serving, toss with onion, spinach, and greens, then season to taste with salt and pepper. Makes 6 servings.

TOSSED GREEN SALAD WITH KIDNEY BEANS AND SPROUTS

4 cups torn spinach leaves
2 cups mixed salad greens (Boston, romaine, iceberg, or escarole)
2 cups bean sprouts, rinsed and drained
2 cups diced Cheddar cheese
1 can (15 ounces) kidney beans, rinsed and drained
1 green pepper, diced
½ cup chopped onion
about ¾ cup vinaigrette

Combine spinach, greens, sprouts, cheese, beans, green pepper, and onion. Toss with as much dressing as needed to coat greens lightly. Serve at once. Makes 6 servings.

TOSSED GREEN SALAD WITH GRAPEFRUIT AND AVOCADO

1 whole grapefruit, peeled and sectioned
1 avocado, halved, peeled, and sliced
3 tablespoons lime juice, divided
6 tablespoons salad oil
½ teaspoon salt
pepper
1 bunch watercress, rinsed and drained
4 cups torn spinach leaves
2 cups sliced Chinese cabbage

Toss grapefruit sections and avocado slices with 1 tablespoon lime juice, cover, and chill. Combine remaining lime juice, the oil, salt, and pepper to taste and set aside. Break tender leaves and stems from watercress and mix with greens; chill. Just before serving, toss greens with dressing. Add grapefruit and avocado and serve at once. Makes 6 servings.

BEAN SPROUT AND CHINESE CABBAGE SALAD

¼ cup mayonnaise
2 tablespoons soy sauce
1 small clove garlic, crushed
dash of sugar
3 cups shredded Chinese cabbage, packed
about 2 cups bean sprouts, rinsed and drained
6 large radishes, sliced
1 green onion with top, minced

In salad bowl, beat well mayonnaise, soy sauce, garlic, and sugar. Add cabbage, sprouts, radishes, and onion; toss lightly to mix. Serve at once. Makes 4 servings.

VARIATION

You may substitute romaine lettuce for all or part of the Chinese cabbage.

GREEK SALAD

2 quarts salad greens, torn (romaine or a mixture of greens)
1 cucumber, peeled and thinly sliced
2 tomatoes, cut in chunks
1 cup cubed Greek feta cheese
12 Greek black olives
½ medium sweet onion, thinly sliced
½ cup julienne beets
6 anchovy fillets, cut in small pieces
1 tablespoon capers
about ½ cup vinaigrette, made with mustard

Put all ingredients except the vinaigrette in a large bowl. Toss with enough dressing to coat everything lightly. Makes 6 servings.

CHERRY TOMATO AND WATERCRESS SALAD

2 cups cherry tomatoes, quartered
4 to 6 cups watercress leaves (2 or 3 bunches)
½ cup vinaigrette
1 cup croutons (optional)

Combine tomatoes and watercress. Toss lightly with enough dressing to coat leaves. Garnish with croutons, if desired. Makes 6 servings.

VARIATION

Mushroom-Cress Salad
Substitute ¼ pound mushrooms, thinly sliced, for cherry tomatoes.

BELGIAN ENDIVE AND MUSHROOM SALAD

4 heads Belgian endive
¼ pound mushrooms, sliced
½ cup vinaigrette

Cut endives in quarters lengthwise and arrange on individual salad plates. Divide mushrooms among plates. Serve with dressing. Makes 4 servings.

Note: Prepare this salad just before serving to avoid discoloration of endives and mushrooms.

ARMENIAN CUCUMBER-SPINACH SALAD

2 cucumbers, unpeeled
1 cup finely sliced celery
½ cup minced parsley (preferably the flat Italian kind)
about 2 quarts tender spinach leaves
½ cup vinaigrette, preferably made with olive oil
pinch of oregano

Seed and dice cucumbers and set aside. Just before serving, blot dry and combine with celery, parsley, and spinach. Toss with just enough dressing to coat leaves. Sprinkle with oregano and serve. Makes 6 servings.

VARIATION

Use romaine lettuce instead of spinach.

ORIENTAL SPINACH SALAD

1 tablespoon white vinegar
1 tablespoon soy sauce
¾ teaspoon sugar
¼ teaspoon ginger
3 tablespoons oil
1 green onion with top, finely minced
6 cups torn spinach leaves
2 cups shredded Chinese cabbage
2 tablespoons toasted sesame seed

In salad bowl, blend vinegar, soy sauce, sugar, and ginger. Stir in oil and onion. Add spinach, cabbage, and sesame seed. Toss lightly to coat. Serve at once. Makes 6 servings.

Slaws

The food processor makes fast work of shredding stubborn vegetables, such as cabbage and carrots; a sharp knife or grater, on the other hand, trades speed for silence. All the slaws in the recipes that follow, whether the creamy or the vinegary kind, benefit from a period of rest before being served.

CABBAGE IN CABBAGE

An elegant presentation for the humble slaw is to serve it in a hollowed-out head of cabbage. Pick a large, handsome Savoy cabbage, one that looks like a great, green, blooming rose.

1 large Savoy cabbage
1 small cabbage
1 to 1½ cups mayonnaise, preferably homemade
1 to 1½ cups sour cream
salt and pepper
lemon juice
hot pepper sauce (optional)
sliced radishes, olives, and hard-cooked eggs for garnish

With a sharp knife and a sure eye, cut out center of large cabbage to form a shell large enough to accommodate salad, about 6 cups. Put in plastic bag and chill. Core and finely shred small cabbage and section removed from large cabbage. Mix with enough mayonnaise and sour cream to make a creamy salad. Season to taste with salt, pepper, lemon juice, and hot pepper sauce if desired. Allow to mellow in refrigerator 1½ to 2 hours. Just before serving, fill cabbage and garnish with remaining ingredients. Makes 8 to 10 servings.

GERMAN CABBAGE SALAD

12 cups finely shredded green or red cabbage (about 3-pound head)
½ cup vegetable oil
⅔ cup cider vinegar
1 teaspoon salt
½ teaspoon pepper
2 tablespoons sugar
2 teaspoons caraway seed

Cover shredded cabbage with boiling water and let stand about 5 minutes; drain. Combine oil with ⅔ cup water and remaining ingredients and mix with cabbage. Let stand 1 hour or longer. (For the ultimate in flavor, make this salad a day in advance: it improves greatly with standing.) Serve cold but not chilled. Makes 12 servings.

CABBAGE-CELERY-CUCUMBER SALAD WITH YOGURT DRESSING

¼ cup yogurt
¼ cup mayonnaise
1 small clove garlic, crushed or minced
½ teaspoon salt
few drops of hot pepper sauce
2 cups shredded green or red cabbage, packed
3 ribs celery, thinly sliced
1 small cucumber, peeled, quartered lengthwise, seeded, and sliced
8 to 10 medium radishes, chopped (½ cup)

In salad bowl, blend yogurt, mayonnaise, garlic, salt, and pepper sauce. Add cabbage, celery, and cucumber; toss to mix well; chill at least ½ hour. Sprinkle with radishes. Makes 4 servings.

CARAWAY CARROT SLAW

⅓ cup buttermilk
⅓ cup mayonnaise
½ teaspoon caraway seed
½ teaspoon salt
⅛ teaspoon pepper
4 cups shredded carrots (1 pound)
½ cup chopped celery (2 small ribs)
3 medium-sized green onions with tops, cut in ½-inch slices
lettuce leaves (optional)

In bowl, mix well buttermilk, mayonnaise, caraway seed, salt, and pepper. Stir in carrots, celery, and onions. Cover and refrigerate at least 1 hour to blend flavors. Serve in lettuce-lined bowl if desired. Makes 6 to 8 servings.

PEAR SLAW

Pear slaw is a wonderful winter salad that goes well with cold-weather favorites, such as roast pork.

1 pound pears
1 tart red apple
2 tablespoons lemon juice
2 cups finely shredded cabbage
¼ cup mayonnaise
¼ teaspoon salt
⅛ teaspoon pepper

Core and dice the pears and apple (do not peel) and drop the pieces into lemon juice. Add the cabbage. Toss with mayonnaise until everything is well coated and season with salt and pepper. Chill for at least 1 hour. Makes 4 to 6 servings.

Vegetable Salads

Not all salads, of course, are green. Raw or cooked vegetables, alone or in felicitous combinations, are a welcome change from leafy greens. The recipes that follow run the gamut from apples to zucchini, with every kind of dressing from silky mild to refreshingly tart.

MAGYAR SALÁTA

This is a salad with zest that shows the Hungarian colors — and flavors.

1 medium green pepper, sliced in thin rings
2 medium tomatoes, sliced ¼-inch thick
* 1 large sweet onion, very thinly sliced
1 tablespoon white vinegar
1 teaspoon sugar
½ teaspoon salt
¼ teaspoon pepper
⅓ cup oil
1 tablespoon minced parsley

Alternate pepper, tomato, and onion slices in shallow glass serving dish. Combine vinegar, 1 tablespoon water, sugar, salt, and pepper; add oil and stir well or shake in screw-top jar. Pour over salad. Chill at least 1 hour before serving. Garnish with parsley. Makes 6 servings.

CELERY ROOT AND POTATO SALAD

The French, Germans, and Swiss all enjoy this kind of celery root and potato salad. It is a pleasant meld of flavors.

1 small celery root
salt
lemon juice
1 pound small new potatoes
2 tablespoons snipped parsley
½ cup mayonnaise
2 tablespoons Dijon mustard
pepper
watercress (optional)

Peel celery root, removing all dark eyes and spots, and cut in ½-inch cubes. Cook in boiling salted water with a few drops of lemon juice 6 to 8 minutes, or until just tender. Cool. Cook potatoes in boiling salted water until just tender. Cool, peel, and dice. Combine with celery root and parsley. Mix mayonnaise and mustard and thin slightly with lemon juice. Toss gently with vegetables. Add salt and freshly ground pepper to taste. Chill. Garnish with watercress, if desired. Makes 6 servings.

WALDORF SALAD

4 tart red eating apples, unpeeled
juice of 1 lemon
1 cup diced celery
½ cup broken walnut meats
½ cup mayonnaise
salt
lettuce leaves

Core and dice the apples and toss them in the lemon juice. Add celery and walnuts. Mix in mayonnaise and season lightly with salt. Arrange on lettuce. Makes 4 to 6 servings.

Note: This is the classic Waldorf salad. You may want to add 1 cup of seedless grapes cut in half, or substitute hazelnuts or even unsalted peanuts for the walnuts.

GEMÜSE SALAT

Gemüse salat is a simple kind of salad often served in German homes and restaurants, even the most elegant ones.

1 cup peas, cooked and drained
1 cup cauliflower, cooked and drained
⅛ pound button mushrooms, sautéed in butter
1 cup asparagus, cut in bite-sized pieces, cooked, and drained
½ cup mayonnaise
½ cup yogurt
½ teaspoon salt
⅛ teaspoon pepper
1 teaspoon prepared mustard
2 drops hot pepper sauce
minced parsley

In large bowl, combine peas, cauliflower flowerets, mushrooms, and asparagus. Mix mayonnaise, yogurt, salt, pepper, mustard, and pepper sauce; pour over vegetables and toss well. Chill well. Garnish with parsley. Makes 4 servings.

Note: You may use any combination of leftover vegetables. Try cooked green beans, beets, carrots, or potatoes. Chopped raw celery is good to add. Garnish with hard-cooked eggs, olives, or tomato slices, if desired.

BROCCOLI AND BERMUDA ONION SALAD

2 cups broccoli buds
½ Bermuda (sweet) onion, cut in quarters and thinly sliced crosswise (about 1 cup)
½ cup vinaigrette
5 cups torn romaine lettuce

Marinate broccoli and onion in dressing at least ½ hour. Just before serving, add lettuce and toss. Makes 6 servings.

CURRIED ASPARAGUS AND MUSHROOM SALAD

¾ cup mayonnaise
3 tablespoons sour cream
1½ teaspoons curry powder
1 teaspoon grated onion
½ teaspoon sugar, or to taste
¾ teaspoon lemon juice, or to taste
salt and pepper
¼ pound mushrooms, stems removed (reserve for other use) and
   caps sliced
2 cups asparagus, cut in 1½-inch pieces, cooked and chilled (1 to
   1½ pounds)
1 tablespoon minced parsley (optional)

Mix well mayonnaise, sour cream, curry powder, and onion. Season to taste with sugar, lemon juice, salt, and pepper. Add mushrooms and asparagus; toss gently until well mixed. Sprinkle with minced parsley, if desired. Makes 4 servings.

FETA-EGGPLANT SALAD

1 medium eggplant (about 1 pound)
1 small onion, chopped
¼ cup olive oil
2 tablespoons lemon juice, or more to taste
salt and pepper
chopped parsley
sliced tomatoes
black olives, preferably oil-cured
green pepper strips
sliced sweet onion
cubes of feta cheese

Wrap whole eggplant in aluminum foil and bake in preheated 400° oven 45 minutes, or until soft. Remove skin and dice eggplant. Add onion, oil, and lemon juice, and salt and pepper to taste; chill. Put on serving plate and sprinkle with parsley. Surround with remaining ingredients. Makes 6 servings.

ZUCCHINI-YOGURT SALAD

    3 zucchini, scrubbed and thinly sliced (about 6 cups)
    2 tablespoons chopped parsley
    3 tablespoons lemon juice
    2 tablespoons salad oil
    ½ teaspoon salt
    pepper
    1 clove garlic, scored
    ½ cup plain yogurt
    3 cups torn salad greens
    ⅓ cup finely chopped radishes
    ⅓ cup black olives, pitted and sliced

Combine zucchini, parsley, lemon juice, oil, salt, pepper to taste, and garlic; cover and chill 1 hour. Discard garlic. Combine zucchini and yogurt and mound on bed of greens. Top with radishes and olives. Makes 6 servings.

BEAN SALAD

    ½ pound (1 cup) dried kidney beans, red or white
    1 small onion, minced
    2 tablespoons finely chopped parsley
    ⅓ cup lemon-oil dressing or vinaigrette
    sliced cucumbers (optional)

Soak and cook beans as described on page 129. Drain and cool. Mix with onion, parsley, and dressing and chill thoroughly. Garnish with cucumber slices, if desired. Makes 6 servings.

Note: You may substitute canned beans for home-cooked beans.

LENTIL SALAD

½ pound dried lentils
½ cup chopped parsley
½ cup minced green onion
1 clove garlic, minced
⅓ cup vinaigrette
salad greens
sliced hard-cooked eggs

In large saucepan, cover washed lentils with 3 cups water. Bring slowly to boil and simmer 30 minutes, or until tender. Drain and chill. Add parsley, onion, and garlic. Stir in vinaigrette dressing. Serve on crisp greens with a garnish of egg slices. Makes 6 servings.

GERMAN-STYLE VEGETABLE SALAD PLATTER

dressing (see recipe below)
2 medium-sized white turnips, peeled and cut in julienne strips (2 cups)
2 cups each finely shredded red and green cabbage
2 small cucumbers, peeled and very thinly sliced (2 cups)
½ pound green beans, cut if desired, cooked, and drained
1 medium onion, minced
2 pounds hot cooked potatoes, preferably new
1 tablespoon vinegar, preferably white
salt and black or white pepper
minced parsley
chopped hard-cooked egg yolk

Prepare dressing; set aside. In separate bowls or plastic bags, place turnips, red cabbage, green cabbage, cucumbers, and green beans. Add 2 tablespoons onion to green beans. Pour ⅓ cup dressing over each vegetable; toss lightly (or tightly seal bags and turn several times to mix). Refrigerate 1 to 2 hours, tossing vegetables or turning bags once or twice. Meanwhile, peel and slice hot potatoes into bowl. Add remaining onion and ⅓ cup dressing, the vinegar, and salt and pepper to taste; toss gently. Let stand 5 to 10 minutes. Mound in center of platter. With slotted spoon, remove marinating vegetables from bowls or bags and arrange in mounds around potato salad. Season to taste with salt and pepper. (Reserve any dressing left in bowls; refrigerate and use for future salads.) Sprinkle potato salad with parsley and other vegetables with egg yolk. This potato salad is best served slightly warm. Makes 6 servings.

Dressing

In bowl or jar with tight-fitting lid, stir or shake well 1 tablespoon sugar, 1 teaspoon salt, black or white pepper to taste, and ⅓ cup each water and vinegar, preferably white. Add 1⅓ cups oil; beat or shake well. Shake before using. Makes 2 cups.

RAITA

This Indian relish, usually served as a foil to curries and other highly spiced dishes, makes a good salad on its own.

    1 teaspoon whole mustard seed
    1 tablespoon butter or vegetable oil
    1 large cucumber, peeled and seeded
    1 cup yogurt
    1 tablespoon lime or lemon juice
    1 teaspoon salt
    dash of pepper
    1 teaspoon snipped Chinese parsley (cilantro or coriander leaves),
          or regular parsley

Put seed in small skillet with butter. Cover and heat until seed pops. Dice or grate cucumber and mix with yogurt. Season to taste with juice, salt, and pepper. Stir in the mustard seed and parsley. Chill for 1 hour. Makes 4 servings.

Note: You may use fresh-snipped mint instead of coriander or parsley leaves.

VEGETABLES WITH SOUR CREAM

1 large tomato, seeded and diced
1 large green pepper, seeded and diced
1 medium cucumber, peeled and diced
¼ cup chopped radishes
4 tablespoons thinly sliced green onions with tops (about 4)
¼ teaspoon salt
dash of pepper
½ to ¾ cup sour cream
½ cup cottage cheese

In large bowl, lightly toss tomato, green pepper, cucumber, radishes, 3 tablespoons onions, salt, and pepper. In small bowl, mix well sour cream and cottage cheese; spoon over vegetables. Garnish with remaining 1 tablespoon onion. Makes 4 servings.

VARIATION

For a low-fat, low-sodium dish, use yogurt instead of sour cream and omit cottage cheese and salt.

CAPONATA

This popular Italian relish-salad will keep for two weeks or more in the refrigerator.

2 large green peppers, seeded and chopped (2 cups)
3 small onions, chopped (about 1½ cups)
½ cup olive oil, divided
4 ribs celery, chopped (about 1½ cups)
2 medium eggplants, diced (6 cups)
2 cans (28 ounces each) tomatoes, coarsely chopped
1 can (16 ounces) pitted black olives, drained, and sliced
1 jar (2 ounces) pitted green olives, drained and sliced
2 tablespoons capers
½ cup vinegar mixed with 2 tablespoons sugar
2 cloves garlic, halved, with toothpick inserted in each piece

In large skillet, sauté peppers and onions in ¼ cup oil until crisp-tender, about 10 minutes, stirring frequently. Add celery and eggplant and cook and stir until eggplant is limp, adding remaining ¼ cup oil as needed. Stir in tomatoes, olives, capers, and ¼ cup vinegar mixture. Cook, uncovered, over low heat 15 minutes. Transfer mixture to large bowl; add remaining vinegar and toss lightly. Bury garlic in mixture. Cover tightly with foil or plastic wrap and store in refrigerator 24 hours to blend flavors. Serve cold. Makes about 10 cups.

BEETS IN WINE

    2 tablespoons butter or margarine
    ¼ cup dry red wine
    3 tablespoons honey
    ¼ teaspoon ground cloves
    ½ teaspoon grated orange rind
    1 can (1 pound) tiny beets, drained

Bring the butter, wine, honey, cloves, and orange rind to a simmer. Add beets and heat through. Let stand at least 15 minutes to blend flavors; serve hot or cold. Makes 4 servings.

Note: You may use cooked fresh beets, whole or sliced ¼-inch thick, in place of canned beets.

MARINATED GREEN BEAN AND CARROT SALAD

    ½ pound green beans, trimmed but left whole
    1 cup carrots, sliced about ¼-inch thick
    ½ cup sliced celery
    3 tablespoons lemon juice
    2 tablespoons oil
    1 tablespoon minced onion
    ½ teaspoon salt
    dash of pepper
    ¼ teaspoon oregano

Steam or parboil the beans and carrots until tender but still crisp; drain. Stir in remaining ingredients, cover, and chill at least 4 hours or overnight, stirring occasionally. Makes 4 servings.

TOMATOES AND OKRA

For this dish, use the smallest okra you can find, what would be called ladies' fingers in Arabic. This is an excellent choice to accompany grilled chicken or lamb.

    1 pound small fresh okra
    ⅓ cup olive oil
    3 or 4 onions, coarsely chopped
    2 cloves garlic, peeled and chopped
    1 can (29 ounces) tomatoes
    salt and pepper
    1 teaspoon ground coriander
    lemon wedges

Trim okra, wash, and dry thoroughly with paper towel. Heat olive oil in large skillet and add onion and garlic. Cook gently until tender. Add okra and cook, tossing lightly, until slightly browned. Add remaining ingredients, except lemon. Cover and simmer until okra is tender, about 30 minutes. Serve cold with lemon wedges. Makes 6 to 8 servings.

Note: If fresh okra is not available, substitute 2 packages (10 ounces each) frozen okra.

PICKLED CUCUMBERS, SCANDINAVIAN STYLE

    2 medium cucumbers, peeled and unpeeled in alternate strips,
        then very thinly sliced
    1 teaspoon salt
    ½ cup white or cider vinegar
    ¼ cup sugar
    dash of hot pepper sauce or pepper
    1 small green onion with top, minced

Put cucumbers in bowl and add salt. Mix well and let stand at room temperature 1 hour or longer to drain out liquid. Drain well. Add vinegar, sugar, pepper sauce or pepper to taste, and green onion. Toss to mix well. Chill at least 1 hour. Makes 4 servings.

VARIATION

To give pickled cucumbers an Oriental fillip, add 2 teaspoons minced ginger root and 2 teaspoons sesame seed to the salad.

PICKLED TURNIPS

1½ pounds small white turnips
2 tablespoons salt
1 cup white vinegar
¾ cup sugar
½ teaspoon yellow food coloring
¼ teaspoon paprika

Peel turnips and cut crosswise in thin slices not more than ¼-inch thick. Mix with the salt and let stand 1 hour. Drain and rinse thoroughly with water. Bring remaining ingredients to boil. Add turnips and simmer 2 minutes. Cool. Makes 8 servings.

LEEKS NIÇOISES

12 to 14 leeks
¼ cup olive oil
5 or 6 tomatoes, peeled and quartered
24 oil-cured black olives, pitted
2 tablespoons lemon juice
1 teaspoon grated lemon rind
salt and pepper
1 tablespoon chopped parsley

Clean leeks thoroughly and cut them in 2-inch lengths. Heat oil in a saucepan and add leeks, turning to coat all pieces. Cover and steam for 10 minutes over low heat. Add the tomatoes, olives, lemon juice, and rind; season with salt and pepper to taste. Cook, covered, 10 to 15 minutes, or until leeks are tender. Cool. Sprinkle with parsley before serving. Makes 6 servings.

MARINATED ZUCCHINI

    4 medium zucchini (about 1½ pounds)
    ½ cup dry white wine
    ⅓ cup oil, preferably olive
    1 teaspoon salt, or to taste
    ½ teaspoon pepper, or to taste
    ⅛ teaspoon tarragon or chervil
    minced parsley (optional)

Cut zucchini in ¾-inch strips. Cut strips diagonally in ½-inch pieces (about 5 cups); set aside. Bring to boil wine, oil, salt, pepper, and tarragon. Add zucchini; bring back to boil. Cover, then simmer until crisp-tender, about 8 minutes, stirring occasionally. Remove to serving dish. Cover and chill thoroughly, several hours. Garnish with parsley. Makes 4 servings.

VARIATION

Other vegetables, such as mushrooms and eggplant, may be prepared in the same way.

BLUE CHEESE MARINATED TOMATOES

    1 tablespoon red wine vinegar
    3 tablespoons salad oil
    ¼ teaspoon salt
    pinch of white pepper
    3 medium tomatoes, cut in chunks
    2 tablespoons coarsely shredded blue cheese, or more to taste

Mix together the vinegar, oil, salt, and pepper and pour over the tomatoes. Let stand ½ hour, then sprinkle with cheese. Makes 3 or 4 servings.

Note: Blue cheese shreds well if kept in the freezer.

TOMATOES FINES HERBES

    3 medium tomatoes, sliced
    2 tablespoons tarragon vinegar or other wine vinegar
    3 tablespoons olive oil
    ½ teaspoon salt
    1 teaspoon chopped fresh tarragon or ¼ teaspoon dried tarragon
    1 tablespoon minced parsley
    1 tablespoon minced chives or white part of green onion
    pepper

Arrange tomato slices in serving dish. Mix remaining ingredients and pour over tomatoes. Let stand at room temperature at least 1 hour before serving. Makes 3 or 4 servings.

Note: For a change of pace, substitute fresh basil for the tarragon.

TOMATOES IN RED ONION MARINADE

    2 tablespoons lemon juice
    ¼ cup salad oil
    ½ teaspoon salt
    pinch of pepper
    1 small red onion, sliced in very thin rings
    3 medium tomatoes, cut in wedges

Combine the lemon juice, oil, salt, and pepper with the onion and let stand for at least ½ hour. Pour over the tomatoes and serve. Makes 3 or 4 servings.

Molded Salads

Few things are as easy on the eye — and the waistline — as a molded salad. Make one in the cool early-morning hours of a hot summer day and watch those wilted appetites perk up at the dinner table.

GAZPACHO SALAD MOLD

    1 envelope unflavored gelatin
    1⅔ cups tomato juice
    2 tablespoons wine vinegar
    1 large tomato, peeled, seeded, and chopped
    1 cucumber, peeled and chopped
    1 canned green chili, well drained, seeded, and chopped
    ¼ cup sliced green onions
    1 clove garlic, minced or mashed
    ¾ teaspoon salt
    ⅛ teaspoon pepper
    pinch of sugar
    crisp salad greens

Soften gelatin in ¼ cup tomato juice. Heat remaining juice. Add softened gelatin and stir until thoroughly dissolved. Add remaining ingredients, except greens, and pour into 4-cup mold. Chill overnight, or until set. Unmold on platter lined with greens. Makes 4 to 6 servings.

MIXED VEGETABLE SALAD

> 2 cups mixed vegetables (such as peas, carrots, green beans,
>   asparagus, broccoli buds), fresh or frozen
> 2 envelopes unflavored gelatin
> 2 cups beef broth
> ¼ cup medium-dry sherry or white wine
> ¼ cup minced red or green pepper
> ¼ cup sliced pimiento-stuffed olives
> crisp salad greens
> lemon wedges

Cook vegetables until crisp-tender; drain and cool. Soften gelatin in ½ cup water in small saucepan. Put over low heat, stirring until dissolved. Add to beef broth and sherry. Stir to mix, then chill until slightly thickened. Fold in cooked vegetables, pepper, and olives. Pour into 4-cup mold. Chill until firm. Unmold on greens and serve with lemon wedges. Makes 6 servings.

CREAMY CUCUMBER-PINEAPPLE SALAD

> 1 small cucumber, peeled, seeded, and chopped (about 2 cups)
> ½ teaspoon salt
> 2 envelopes unflavored gelatin
> 1¼ cups pineapple juice
> ¼ cup cider vinegar
> 2 tablespoons sugar
> ⅛ teaspoon dill weed, slightly crushed
> ½ cup sour cream
> 1 can (8¼ ounces) crushed pineapple, drained
> cherry tomatoes

Sprinkle cucumber with salt and let stand at least 15 minutes. Drain well. Meanwhile, soften gelatin in ½ cup cold water in saucepan and put over low heat, stirring until dissolved. Add juice, vinegar, sugar, dill weed, and sour cream, stir to blend, then chill until slightly thickened. Fold in cucumber and pineapple, pour into 5-cup ring mold, and chill until firm. Unmold and fill center with cherry tomatoes. Makes 6 to 8 servings.

Potato Salads

TIPS FOR PERFECT POTATO SALAD

• Use only red or white new potatoes or California long whites. All-purpose and baking potatoes crumble and lose their shape.

• Boil the potatoes in their skins (scrubbed first, of course) until they are barely tender. Drain them and let them stand until they are cool enough to handle. Peel and slice them about ¼-inch thick.

• Prepare the dressing while the potatoes are cooking. Toss the potatoes gently just until all the pieces are coated.

• Let the salad rest awhile before serving to give the potatoes time to absorb some of the dressing. Warm salads can be left at room temperature for about one hour; cold salads should be refrigerated for several hours or even overnight.

• Always refrigerate salads that contain mayonnaise: it can spoil quickly in a warm kitchen.

FRENCH-STYLE POTATO SALAD

about 1½ pounds red or white new potatoes
3 tablespoons vinegar
6 tablespoons salad oil
½ teaspoon salt
pepper
3 tablespoons each chopped parsley and green onion

Boil unpeeled potatoes until tender. Drain and let stand at room temperature until cool enough to handle. Meanwhile, combine vinegar, oil, salt, and pepper to taste; add parsley and green onion. Peel potatoes and cut in thin slices; make shallow layers in mixing bowl, sprinkling each with some of dressing. Let stand an hour or so at room temperature, tossing once or twice very carefully so potatoes do not crumble. Serve at room temperature. Makes 6 servings.

Note: To give your salad an authentic French cachet, use white wine vinegar and olive oil.

CREAMY POTATO SALAD

> 1 quart diced cooked potatoes, peeled and still warm (about 2 pounds)
> 1 medium onion, finely chopped (½ cup)
> ½ cup diced celery
> ½ cup diced cucumber
> ½ cup thinly sliced radishes
> 1 tablespoon chopped chives
> 4 hard-cooked eggs, divided
> 1 cup sour cream
> ¼ cup mayonnaise
> ½ teaspoon salt
> ⅛ teaspoon pepper
> dash of cayenne
> 2 tablespoons vinegar or lemon juice
> ½ teaspoon Dijon mustard

Combine potatoes, onion, celery, cucumber, radishes, and chives. Dice whites of 3 eggs and add to vegetables. In bowl mash 3 egg yolks with fork; stir in sour cream, mayonnaise, salt, pepper, cayenne, vinegar or lemon juice, and mustard. Add to vegetables and mix well. Garnish with remaining egg, sliced. Chill several hours. Makes 6 to 8 servings.

HOT GERMAN POTATO SALAD

about 1½ pounds new potatoes, preferably red
salt
¼ pound slab bacon, diced in ¼-inch cubes
1 medium onion, finely chopped (½ cup)
2 tablespoons flour
1 tablespoon sugar
dash of pepper
⅓ cup cider vinegar
3 tablespoons minced parsley

Cook potatoes in boiling salted water until tender. Meanwhile, sauté bacon in a saucepan until crisp. Remove with slotted spoon and set aside; discard all but 2 tablespoons drippings. Sauté onions until soft and golden; do not brown. Stir in flour, sugar, 1 teaspoon salt, and pepper. Dilute vinegar with ⅓ cup water and gradually blend in. Stir over medium heat until mixture thickens and comes to a boil; remove from heat. When potatoes are done, drain well, peel if desired, and slice ¼-inch thick into bowl. Pour the sauce over the potatoes, add all but 1 tablespoon bacon, and toss gently. Garnish with remaining bacon and parsley. Makes 4 to 6 servings.

Note: If slab bacon is not available, use breakfast bacon cut in ⅜-inch squares.

POTATO AND GREEN BEAN SALAD

1 pound warm green beans, cooked and cut
4 warm large potatoes, cooked, peeled, and cubed (about 4 cups)
1 small red onion, thinly sliced
¼ cup oil
2 tablespoons white wine vinegar
1 medium clove garlic, crushed
2 green onions, sliced
1½ teaspoons fresh oregano, minced, or ½ teaspoon dried oregano
1 teaspoon salt
⅛ teaspoon pepper
lettuce leaves (optional)

Place beans, potatoes, and red onion in bowl. In jar, mix well oil, vinegar, garlic, green onions, oregano, salt, and pepper; pour over vegetables. Toss gently; mix well. Cover and chill several hours or overnight. Serve in lettuce-lined bowl, if desired. Makes 4 to 6 servings.

MEDITERRANEAN-STYLE POTATO SALAD

¼ cup minced onion
4 cups diced cooked potato, warm
3 cups diced unpeeled zucchini
½ pound fresh mushrooms, sliced
1 tomato, diced
½ cup olive oil
1½ tablespoons lemon juice
1 tablespoon fresh minced basil leaves
1 teaspoon fresh minced oregano or ¼ teaspoon dried oregano
1¼ teaspoons salt
½ teaspoon coarse black pepper
¼ cup pine nuts

Combine onion, potatoes, zucchini, mushrooms, and tomato in large bowl. In a small bowl or screw-top jar, make a sauce with the olive oil, lemon juice, basil, oregano, salt, and pepper; pour over vegetables and mix well. Chill thoroughly. Just before serving, sprinkle with nuts. Makes 8 servings.

CURRIED POTATO SALAD

⅓ cup chicken broth
2 to 3 teaspoons curry powder
4 warm large potatoes, cooked and cubed (4 cups)
6 green onions with some tops, minced (⅓ cup)
1 teaspoon salt
½ cup mayonnaise
2 tablespoons lemon juice
6 inner ribs celery, thinly sliced (1½ cups)
1 medium-sized tart apple, diced (1 cup)

In small saucepan, heat broth; blend in curry powder. Cook 1 to 2 minutes; cool slightly. In bowl, toss potatoes gently with onions, curry-broth mixture, and salt; let stand until most of broth is absorbed. Mix mayonnaise, lemon juice, celery, and apple. Add to potato mixture. Toss gently to coat. Cover and chill at least 2 hours. Makes 6 servings.

5

MEATLESS
MAIN DISHES

You don't have to be a vegetarian to appreciate a meatless meal. Whether it is a Della Robbia wreath of hot or cold vegetables served with an assortment of dips or an array of elegant stuffed vegetables, the sight alone can make your mouth begin to water.

Cooking without meat (or poultry or fish) does not require any special knowledge or skills, though perhaps you should pay more attention than usual to appearances. Color and shape play a big role in determining appeal. Texture, too, counts a lot when you are deciding which vegetables to put together in a stir-fry or how to join them up with pasta or eggs.

The recipes in this chapter, which is the longest in the book, are arranged in categories: vegetable platters; stir-fry vegetables; fritters; casseroles, medleys, and curry; stuffed vegetables; dried beans and legumes; pasta; dumplings; omelets; soufflés; quiches; and salads. We hope that in some of the categories, readers will feel encouraged to create their own recipes. For example, there are no hard-and-fast rules about what to put on a vegetable platter or in a stir-fry; there can't be. The choice depends on availability, cost, compatibility, and above all, the preferences of the people who are going to be eating it. Only the person on the scene can make these judgments, and that person is the cook. On the other hand, there isn't much margin for error in soufflés or dumplings, so the directions in those categories are quite specific.

There are enough recipes in this chapter to keep a family going for a couple of months. Not everyone will want to do that — and those who do should be sure they are meeting their protein needs — but even one or two meatless meals a week can make a significant difference in the budget. What is more, when such meals depend on vegetables, the needle on the bathroom scale often goes down as well.

Vegetable Platters

The first — and last — word in vegetable main dishes is an array of hot or cold fresh vegetables assembled with a feel for flavors and textures and an eye to appearance. While the selection and quantity are flexible, there can be no compromise when it comes to quality.

HOT VEGETABLE PLATTER

> 3 tablespoons butter or margarine
> 4 to 6 small new potatoes, cooked, drained, and kept warm
> ½ pound green beans, cooked, drained, and kept warm
> 2 medium zucchini, cut diagonally in ¼-inch slices
> oil
> 1 small eggplant (¾ pound), cut in ¾-inch fingers
> about 16 cherry tomatoes
> salt and pepper
> 2 hard-cooked eggs, halved
> mustard sauce (see recipe below)
> minced parsley (optional)

Add 1 tablespoon butter to potatoes in saucepan; cover and set aside. Add 1 tablespoon butter to beans in saucepan; cover and set aside. Cook zucchini in 1 tablespoon oil in covered heavy saucepan over medium heat until crisp-tender, about 6 minutes, shaking pan occasionally; set aside. Heat ¼ cup oil in large heavy skillet until hot. Add eggplant and fry until well browned on all sides and almost tender, adding more oil if necessary. Remove and drain on paper towels. Add remaining 1 tablespoon butter to skillet and sauté tomatoes, shaking skillet gently, until tomatoes are heated and glazed but still keep their shape, about 3 minutes (do not overcook). Push to one side of skillet. Add eggplant to other side and reheat. Also, if necessary, quickly reheat potatoes, zucchini, and beans over low heat. Season with salt and pepper to taste. Arrange vegetables and eggs attractively on large heated platter. Drizzle with some mustard sauce. Sprinkle with parsley. Pass remaining sauce. Makes 4 servings.

Mustard Sauce

Season 1½ cups medium white sauce with 1 teaspoon prepared mustard and salt and pepper to taste.

VARIATION

If desired, substitute sliced or quartered cooked beets for potatoes. Reheat with 1 tablespoon butter and 1 teaspoon lemon juice; season with salt and pepper to taste.

COLD VEGETABLE PLATTER

⅓ cup cooked dried beans per serving
tomatoes, cut in ⅜-inch slices, or whole cherry tomatoes
green peppers, cut in thin rings or strips
green onions, white parts plus about 1 inch of green
carrots, cut in sticks or grated
celery sticks
fennel, cut in ¼-inch slices
kohlrabi, sliced ¼ inch or thinner
white turnip, very thinly sliced or grated
radishes, sliced, cut in roses, or whole with 1 inch of green
cauliflower (raw or parboiled), broken into flowerets
broccoli (raw or parboiled), broken into flowerets
zucchini, diagonally sliced in ¼-inch pieces
cucumbers, very thinly sliced
beets (cooked), sliced ¼-inch thick
sugar-snap peas, whole
snow peas, whole
green beans, whole
mushrooms, sliced ¼-inch thick and rubbed with lemon
avocado, sliced and rubbed with lemon

Arrange as many vegetables as you need and have on hand on platters and serve them with one or more dips. Balance crunchy vegetables with softer ones, sharp flavors with mellow. Think of colors and shapes, too, as you plan your platters. Make the meal as good to look at as it is to eat.

DIPS

Herb-Yogurt Dip

> 1 teaspoon caraway seed
> 1 cup plain yogurt
> 1 tablespoon chopped green onion
> 1 teaspoon fresh minced basil, or ¼ teaspoon dried crushed basil

Pour boiling water over caraway seed, let stand about 5 minutes, then drain. Add to yogurt with green onion and basil. Chill several hours. Makes 1 cup.

Yogurt-Vegetable Dip

> ½ cup creamed cottage cheese
> 1 tablespoon finely grated carrot
> 2 teaspoons finely grated onion
> 1 teaspoon finely chopped green pepper
> ½ teaspoon salt
> dash of pepper
> 1 cup yogurt

With fork, beat cottage cheese in small bowl. Add carrot, onion, green pepper, salt, and pepper and mix well. Fold in yogurt, cover, and chill. Makes 1½ cups.

Guacamole

> 1 ripe avocado
> juice of 1 lime or lemon
> salt
> dash of hot pepper sauce

Peel and seed avocado, mash with fork, and blend in as much juice as needed for dip consistency. Mixture should not be smooth. Stir in salt and hot pepper sauce to taste. Makes 1 cup.

Mock Aioli Dip

In Provence, aioli is made by crushing as much as half a head of garlic in a mortar and building an olive oil mayonnaise on it. Here is a simpler, less powerful version of the real thing.

    1 cup mayonnaise
    1 tablespoon lemon juice
    3 large cloves garlic, crushed in a garlic press
    salt and pepper

Blend all the ingredients well; cover and chill at least 1 hour. Serve at room temperature. Makes 1 cup.

Curry Mayonnaise

    1 cup mayonnaise, preferably homemade
    1 tablespoon lemon juice
    1 tablespoon grated fresh ginger root
    1 clove garlic, minced
    1 tablespoon curry powder
    dash of hot pepper sauce or cayenne, or to taste

Put all the ingredients in a blender or food processor and blend well. Makes about 1 cup.

Horseradish Dip

    1 cup sour cream
    ¼ to ⅓ cup horseradish, or to taste
    ½ teaspoon grated lemon peel
    1 teaspoon lemon juice
    dash of pepper
    dash of hot pepper sauce

Blend all ingredients, taste for seasoning, cover, and chill. Makes about 1 cup.

Roquefort-Walnut Dip

This dip is particularly good with fennel, celery, or green pepper strips as well as with apple wedges.

> 1 small package (3 ounces) cream cheese
> 1 ounce Roquefort cheese, crumbled
> 1 tablespoon brandy (optional)
> ¼ cup chopped walnuts

Using a food processor or electric mixer, whip cream cheese until fluffy, then beat in Roquefort. Mix in brandy, if desired; stir in nuts. Makes about 1 cup.

Note: You may use blue cheese instead of Roquefort.

Cream Cheese, Radish, and Chive Dip

> 1 package (8 ounces) cream cheese
> 3 tablespoons sour cream or buttermilk
> 1 teaspoon lemon juice
> 6 radishes, peeled and finely chopped
> 2 teaspoons finely chopped chives
> salt and pepper

Beat cream cheese until fluffy, using a food processor or mixer; then beat in sour cream or buttermilk and lemon juice. Stir in radishes and chives; add salt and pepper to taste. Chill 1 hour. Makes about 2 cups.

Note: This dip is also excellent as a spread for crackers or dark bread.

Blue Cheese and Mushroom Dip

> 6 ounces blue cheese
> ¾ cup light cream
> 1 tablespoon chopped chives
> 1 tablespoon minced parsley
> ½ cup chopped fresh mushrooms

Crumble blue cheese and beat in enough cream to get a lumpy dip. Stir in other ingredients and chill for 1 hour. Makes about 2 cups.

Stir-Fry Vegetables

Stir-fry vegetables are a culinary treasure from the Orient that is quick, nutritious, and economical. Vegetables may be prepared individually or in combination, with meat or fish or alone, according to appetites and availability. Serve them with rice for a satisfying main dish.

For successful stir-frying, it is essential to have all the ingredients ready before you start to fry. The oil must be very hot and the vegetables cut so that none takes more than 7 minutes to reach the crisp-tender stage. Cut the vegetables in various shapes, as indicated below, and arrange them on a platter in order of cooking time, from root vegetables to leafy greens.

¼- x 2-inch matchsticks: carrots, parsnips, rutabaga, winter squash, celery root.

⅛-inch slices: sweet potato, Jerusalem artichokes, water chestnuts, turnips.

¼-inch diagonal slices: stems of asparagus, broccoli, and cauliflower; celery stalks.

¼-inch slices: zucchini, mushrooms, tofu (bean curd), radishes.

½-inch slices: green beans (diagonal), green pepper.

½-inch fingers: eggplant.

2-inch pieces: scallions (white and green parts).

Whole pieces: Snow peas, sugar-snap peas, asparagus tips, cauliflower and broccoli flowerets.

Torn pieces: Swiss chard, spinach, and other greens.

BASIC STIR-FRY VEGETABLES

about 12 cups prepared vegetables
2 tablespoons oil
½ teaspoon salt
¼-inch slice of ginger root, peeled and smashed with the flat side
of a cleaver or kitchen knife
1 clove garlic, smashed
thickening sauce (see recipe below)

Prepare vegetables for stir-frying. Heat wok or skillet until red-hot. Swirl oil around pan and immediately add salt, ginger, and garlic. Stir constantly; do not let brown. When the sizzling stops, remove garlic and ginger and add first vegetable. Stir. Cook briefly, stirring constantly, then add remaining vegetables, one by one, according to time needed to cook. When they are still brightly colored and crisp-tender, push to sides of pan and pour in sauce. Stir vegetables back in and cook 1 minute, or until thickened. Serve at once. Makes 6 servings.

Thickening Sauce
Mix together ¼ cup soy sauce, 2 tablespoons sherry, 2 teaspoons sugar, and 1 tablespoon cornstarch. Set aside until ready to use.

Fritters

Virtually any vegetable can be stirred or dipped in a basic fritter batter and fried in hot oil. Try a *fritto misto,* or mixed fry, a combination of different shapes and textures on a platter with several dips and sauces.

Some fritters are like patties or balls; others retain the shape of the dipped vegetable, more or less. For the flat or round kind, stir about 1½ cups cooked vegetables, such as corn, peas, or spinach, into the batter and fry in ½ inch of hot oil. (Deep-fry the fritters to get puffs.) Pieces of parboiled broccoli, cauliflower, parsnips, or green beans may be dipped in batter and fried. Try raw zucchini or eggplant fingers, or whole mushrooms or sugar-snap peas, or strips of green pepper, celery, or fennel. Even raw spinach leaves are delicious batter-fried. For best results, always have the oil very hot and never crowd the pan.

BASIC FRITTERS

> 3 eggs, separated
> oil
> 3 tablespoons flour
> ½ teaspoon salt
> liquid (water, white wine, or flat beer)
> vegetables

Beat the egg yolks together with 1 tablespoon oil; stir in the flour and salt. Add just enough liquid to make a thick, creamy batter. Beat the egg whites until stiff and fold them in. Stir or dip the vegetables in batter and drop in hot oil. Cook until golden brown; drain on paper towels, and serve at once. Makes 4 servings as a main dish, 6 servings as a side dish.

Casseroles, Medleys, and Curry

In those parts of the world where meat is scarce and sunshine is plentiful, certain traditional vegetable combinations have evolved. Some, such as *djuvecs*, the Basque *pipérade*, and Hungarian *lécso*, start with onions, green peppers, and tomatoes. Indeed, any vegetables that are in season simultaneously have probably been put together at some time or place in history, for cooking with vegetables is definitely an improvisational art.

LIMA-BROCCOLI CASSEROLE

1 small bunch broccoli or 1 package (10 ounces) frozen broccoli spears

1½ cups shelled fresh lima beans or 1 package (10 ounces) frozen lima beans

1 can (16 ounces) tomatoes, drained and cut up (reserve juice)

1 cup shredded Cheddar cheese

1 onion, chopped

4 tablespoons butter or margarine

2 tablespoons flour

½ teaspoon salt

¼ teaspoon each pepper and marjoram

1 cup soft bread crumbs

3 tablespoons grated Parmesan cheese

Cook the broccoli and lima beans until barely tender and drain, reserving the cooking liquid. Arrange them in a greased 12 x 8 x 2-inch baking dish. Top with tomatoes and sprinkle with Cheddar cheese. Sauté onion in 2 tablespoons butter until tender. Blend in flour, salt, pepper, and marjoram until smooth. Combine juice from tomatoes and cooking liquid to make 1 cup, adding water if necessary. Gradually stir into onion mixture and cook and stir until thick; pour over vegetables. Melt remaining 2 tablespoons butter and toss with bread crumbs; sprinkle on vegetables and top with Parmesan. Cover with foil and bake in preheated 425° oven 15 minutes, or until bubbly. Remove foil and bake 5 minutes longer to brown. Makes 4 servings.

EGGPLANT AND CHEESE, GREEK STYLE

    1 large eggplant
    salt
    oil
    1 cup chopped onion
    1 clove garlic, crushed
    1 can (1 pound) tomatoes, cut up
    2 tablespoons parsley
    ⅛ teaspoon pepper
    ⅛ teaspoon cinnamon
    1½ cups ricotta or cottage cheese
    ½ cup grated Parmesan cheese
    1 egg

Peel eggplant and slice it ½-inch thick, sprinkle with salt, and set aside for 20 minutes. Wipe dry and fry in hot oil until lightly browned. Remove and drain on paper towels. Add more oil if needed and sauté onion and garlic until onion is tender. Add tomatoes, parsley, pepper, cinnamon and ½ teaspoon salt. Simmer uncovered, 5 minutes. Spread half the tomato mixture in 12 x 8 x 2-inch baking dish. Mix ricotta or cottage cheese, ¼ cup Parmesan, and the egg; spread over tomato mixture. Arrange eggplant, slightly overlapping, on cheese mixture. Sprinkle with remaining Parmesan. Bake, uncovered, in preheated 375° oven 35 to 40 minutes, or until eggplant is tender. Makes 4 servings.

EGGPLANT-POTATO CURRY

3 medium potatoes, peeled and cut in 2-inch chunks
about ¼ cup oil
2 medium eggplants (about 1 pound each), peeled and cut in
2-inch chunks
1 onion, minced
3 medium cloves garlic, crushed
1 tablespoon curry powder (see note)
1 teaspoon salt

In large skillet, sauté potatoes in hot oil over medium heat until light brown; remove and set aside. In same skillet, sauté eggplants, stirring to prevent sticking and adding more oil if necessary, until half-done, 10 to 15 minutes. Remove and set aside. In same pan, sauté onion, garlic, curry powder, and salt 5 minutes, sprinkling with a little water occasionally to prevent burning. Add potatoes and ¾ cup water; cover and cook, stirring occasionally, until potatoes are almost tender, about 10 minutes. Stir in eggplants; cover and simmer, stirring occasionally, 15 to 20 minutes, or until vegetables are tender (add more water if necessary). Makes 2 servings as a main dish, 4 to 6 as a side dish.

Note: Substitute blend of 1 tablespoon ground coriander, ½ teaspoon ground cumin, 1 teaspoon paprika, and ¼ teaspoon turmeric for curry powder, if desired.

COLACHE

Colache is a summer vegetable medley.

2 tablespoons oil
2 medium zucchini, cut in ⅛-inch slices
1 medium green pepper, coarsely chopped
6 large green onions with tops, thinly sliced
1 large clove garlic, crushed
about 2½ cups corn kernels (4 or 5 medium ears)
2 medium tomatoes, peeled and diced
1 teaspoon salt

½ teaspoon sugar
½ teaspoon pepper
½ teaspoon ground cumin
½ cup shredded jack or Cheddar cheese

Heat oil in heavy saucepan or Dutch oven. Add zucchini, green pepper, ½ cup onions, and the garlic. Stir over medium-high heat until vegetables are coated with oil, about 2 minutes. Stir in corn, tomatoes, salt, sugar, pepper, and cumin. Cover and simmer until vegetables are tender, about 12 minutes, stirring occasionally. Sprinkle with cheese and remaining sliced onion tops. Makes 4 servings.

Stuffed Vegetables

Stuffing vegetables is an ancient method of making a little go a long way, with admirable results. Any number of vegetables can be stuffed — with other vegetables or with grains, meat, fish, or cheese, alone or in combination — and they can be presented hot or cold. Besides using eggplant, squash, tomatoes, green peppers, and cabbage, all of which are fairly easy to handle, you can stuff onions, turnips and kohlrabi (parboiled and hollowed out), pumpkins, artichokes, cucumbers, baked potatoes, lettuce, and grape leaves.

SUMMER SQUASH WITH CHEESE STUFFING

> 4 medium yellow or green summer squash (about 2 pounds)
> salt
> 1 medium onion, minced
> 1 tablespoon olive oil
> about ⅓ cup grated Parmesan cheese
> 1 cup diced mozzarella cheese (about 4 ounces)
> ½ cup cracker meal or bread crumbs
> 1 egg
> 1 teaspoon minced fresh basil, or ¼ teaspoon dried basil
> pepper

Parboil squash in boiling salted water for 8 to 10 minutes, or until barely tender. At same time, sauté onion in oil until soft. Remove squash, cut in half lengthwise, and cool slightly. Scoop out pulp, chop it coarsely, and add to onion mixture. Mix in ¼ cup grated Parmesan, ½ teaspoon salt, the mozzarella, cracker meal or bread crumbs, egg, basil, and pepper to taste. Fill squash shells, rounding tops. Arrange in shallow baking dish; sprinkle with remaining grated cheese. Bake in preheated 350° oven 25 to 30 minutes. Makes 4 servings.

VARIATION

Eggplant with Cheese Stuffing
Small or baby eggplants may be prepared the same way. Cut the eggplants in half, remove flesh, and chop it coarsely. Sprinkle pulp and inside of shells with salt and set aside for 20 minutes. Squeeze liquid from pulp and add it to onions; complete filling. Wipe shells dry, fill with cheese mixture, and bake.

TOMATOES WITH WALNUT-RICE STUFFING

    1 cup chopped onion
    2 tablespoons olive oil
    1 cup rice
    ¼ cup minced parsley
    1¾ cups water
    juice of 1 lemon
    1 teaspoon salt
    ½ teaspoon oregano
    ¼ teaspoon thyme
    ⅛ teaspoon pepper
    1 cup chopped walnuts
    6 tablespoons wheat germ
    12 medium tomatoes
    1 cup shredded Swiss cheese

In large skillet, sauté onion in oil until tender. Stir in rice, parsley, water, lemon juice, salt, oregano, thyme, and pepper. Bring to boil, cover, then simmer over low heat 15 minutes. Stir in walnuts and wheat germ. Scoop out tomatoes and add flesh to rice mixture; stuff tomato shells. Place in shallow baking dish and sprinkle with cheese. Bake uncovered in preheated 350° oven 30 minutes, or until heated. Makes 4 servings as a main dish, 6 to 8 as a side dish.

VARIATIONS

Eggplant or Zucchini with Walnut-Rice Stuffing

Halve lengthwise 3 medium eggplants or 6 medium zucchini. Parboil in boiling water to cover 8 to 10 minutes, or until crisp-tender. Drain. Scoop out flesh, leaving ¼-inch shells. Chop flesh, mix with rice mixture, and stuff shells. Place in shallow baking dish; sprinkle with cheese. Add water just to cover bottom of dish. Cover with foil; bake in preheated 350° oven 10 to 15 minutes, or until hot and tender.

Green Peppers with Walnut-Rice Stuffing

Core 12 medium green peppers and parboil in water to cover 8 to 10 minutes, or until crisp-tender. Drain. Stuff with rice mixture. Place in shallow baking dish and sprinkle with cheese. If desired, spoon on 1 can (16 ounces) tomato sauce. Bake uncovered in preheated 350° oven 25 to 30 minutes, or until bubbly and tender.

Cabbage with Walnut-Rice Stuffing

Core 1 medium head (2 to 3 pounds) cabbage and parboil in water to cover 5 minutes or until leaves are slightly wilted and easy to remove; drain in colander. Add cheese to rice mixture and place about ¼ cup on each leaf; fold in sides and roll up; set aside. (Any leftover cabbage can be coarsely shredded and cooked with rolls or saved for future use.) In large kettle, bring to boil 1 can (16 ounces) tomato sauce, 1 cup packed brown sugar, and ½ cup each raisins and lemon juice. Taste: the sauce should be pleasantly sweet-and-sour. Add cabbage rolls, reduce heat, and simmer, uncovered, 25 to 30 minutes, basting occasionally.

POTATOES CÔTE D'OR

These stuffed potatoes are like those served at a famous inn in Burgundy and are a good brunch idea.

    2 large baking potatoes
    1 tablespoon butter
    ¼ cup finely diced cooked ham (optional)

2 tablespoons minced celery, sautéed in a little butter
béchamel sauce (see recipe below)
salt, pepper, and marjoram
4 eggs, poached
grated Parmesan cheese

Scrub potatoes and bake in 400° oven for 1 hour, or until done. Cool slightly and cut in half lengthwise. Scoop out most of pulp, leaving ¼-inch shell. With fork, mash pulp with butter, ham, celery, ¼ cup sauce, and the seasonings. Mix until smooth and pile into shells. Make a depression in top of each with back of spoon. Set potatoes in shallow baking pan and slip an egg into each depression. Coat generously with remaining sauce and sprinkle tops with grated cheese. Bake in preheated 350° oven 10 minutes, or until hot and flecked with gold. Makes 4 servings.

Béchamel Sauce
Melt 2 tablespoons butter and blend in 2 tablespoons flour. Gradually add 1 cup hot milk or ½ cup milk and ½ cup broth. Cook, stirring, until smooth and thickened. Season with salt, pepper, and nutmeg. Makes 1 cup.

TOMATOES STUFFED WITH LENTIL SALAD

1 pound lentils
1 onion, stuck with 2 cloves
1 bay leaf
1 cup thinly sliced green onions
½ cup chopped parsley
1½ tablespoons lemon juice, or more to taste
½ cup oil
salt
8 to 10 medium-large tomatoes
watercress or other greens
8 to 10 cherry tomatoes

Combine lentils, whole onion, bay leaf, and water to cover in heavy kettle. Bring to boil, then reduce heat and simmer, partly covered, until lentils are just soft to the bite, about 30 to 35 minutes (do not overcook). Drain, discard onion, cloves, and bay leaf, and cool thoroughly. Combine with green onions and parsley. Make a dressing with lemon juice and oil, salted to taste. Use as much as needed to moisten lentils well. Remove tops from tomatoes and scoop out pulp with teaspoon, leaving a shell. Sprinkle lightly with salt and set cut side down on paper towels to drain. Fill tomatoes with lentil salad and arrange on serving plate. Garnish with greens and put a cherry tomato in center of each. Makes 8 to 10 servings.

Dried Beans and Legumes

Beans are a marvelous food: they are wholesome, nutritious, economical, and exceedingly versatile. They are enjoyed all over the world. They can be seasoned and spiced in an endless variety of ways and combined with other, fresh vegetables. And since beans supply the body with needed protein when served with a complementary grain, such as rice, they are an invaluable alternative to meat.

TIPS FOR COOKING BEANS

• Cooking dried beans is easy, but it does take time. In most cases, they must be soaked. (Black-eyed peas, lentils, and split peas do *not* require soaking.) Use 2½ to 3 cups water or other liquid for each cup of dried beans. There are two methods:

1. Let beans soak in water at room temperature overnight.

2. In a saucepan, bring beans and water to boil and boil 2 minutes. Remove from heat, cover, and let stand 1 hour.

• After soaking, cook beans as specified in desired recipe. Or place them in heavy saucepan, cover, and simmer with soaking liquid until tender. Suggested times are given below.

• A pressure cooker will save considerable time and fuel. Follow manufacturer's directions for use.

• Beans may also be cooked in a slow cooker 10 to 12 hours at low heat, 5 to 6 hours at high heat. Follow manufacturer's directions.

• Add salt near the end of the cooking time to prevent beans from hardening.

• Always season beans with vinegar or lemon juice (1 tablespoon or more per pound of beans) to aid digestion.

• One pound of beans will make 8 generous servings.

SUGGESTED COOKING TIMES

Bean or legume	In pot on range (hours)	In pressure cooker (minutes) at 15 pounds	at 10 pounds
Black-eyed peas	½	6 to 10	15
Lentils	½	6 to 10	15
Split peas	½	6 to 10	15
Pink beans	¾	10	20
Small limas	¾	10	20
Brown beans	1 to 1½	10 to 15	25 to 30
Chickpeas	1 to 1½	10 to 15	25 to 30
Great northern beans	1 to 1½	10 to 15	25 to 30
Large limas	1 to 1½	10 to 15	25 to 30
Whole peas	1 to 1½	10 to 15	25 to 30
Navy beans	2	10	20
Pinto beans	2	10	20
Black beans	2	10 to 15	25 to 30
Kidney beans	2	10 to 15	25 to 30
Red beans	2	10 to 15	25 to 30
Soybeans	2	25 to 30	50 to 60

LOUISIANA RED BEANS AND RICE

1 pound dried red kidney beans
¼ cup oil
2 cloves garlic, minced
2 medium onions, chopped
2 ribs celery, chopped
¼ cup chopped parsley
1 to 2 tablespoons vinegar
salt
steamed rice

Wash and drain beans, then soak overnight or by the short-soak method (see page 129). Bring to boil, cover, and simmer until beans are barely tender, about 1½ hours, adding more water if needed to keep them covered. Add oil, garlic, onions, celery, and parsley and simmer about ½ hour or until beans are very tender (mixture should be a little juicy). Season to taste with vinegar and salt. Serve beans on mounds of rice. Makes 8 servings.

KIDNEY BEANS, INDIAN STYLE

> 1 pound dried red kidney beans
> ¼ cup oil
> ½ cup chopped onion (1 medium onion)
> 3 cloves garlic, crushed
> ½ teaspoon grated fresh ginger
> ½ teaspoon paprika
> ¼ teaspoon red pepper flakes
> ¼ teaspoon cardamom
> salt
> 3 tablespoons lemon juice
> lemon wedges
> chapati (see recipe below)

Wash and drain beans and soak them overnight or by short-soak method (see page 129). Bring again to boil and simmer, adding more water if necessary, until nearly tender, about 1½ hours. Heat oil, add onion and garlic, and sauté until lightly browned. Add spices and combine with beans. Add salt to taste and simmer 30 minutes, or until liquid has almost evaporated but beans are still juicy. Stir in lemon juice to taste and add more salt if needed. Garnish with lemon wedges and serve with chapati. Makes 8 servings.

Note: You can use 2 cans (1 pound each) kidney beans, rinsed and drained, in place of cooked beans. Cook only long enough for beans to warm through, about 10 minutes, adding a bit of water if needed to keep them from scorching.

Chapati

Mix 3¾ cups whole wheat flour and 1 teaspoon salt in bowl. Add 1½ cups water, or enough to make a soft dough. Put on lightly floured board and knead 5 minutes. Cover with damp cloth and let stand 1 hour. Knead well again. Break off small pieces of dough and shape in balls about the size of a walnut. On lightly floured board, roll each ball very thin. Heat ungreased griddle or heavy skillet and cook on both sides, pressing gently with pancake turner until chapati blister. Remove when lightly browned and crisp. Serve plain or with butter. Makes about 30.

Note: Bread can be made ahead and reheated. Recipe can be halved.

BLACK BEANS AND RICE, CUBAN STYLE

For reasons having more to do with appearance than with history or ideology, this dish is usually called *moros y cristianos*, "Moors and Christians."

½ pound dried black beans
1 medium onion, finely chopped
1 green pepper, finely chopped
1 or 2 cloves garlic, minced
¼ teaspoon thyme leaves
½ bay leaf
¼ cup olive oil
1 to 2 teaspoons vinegar
salt and pepper
chopped sweet onion
steamed rice

Rinse and drain beans and soak, using either the long- or short-soak method (see page 129). Bring to the boil, cover, and simmer until barely tender, about 1½ hours. Sauté next five ingredients in the oil over low heat, stirring occasionally, about 10 minutes. Add to beans and simmer about ½ hour, or until beans are very tender and sauce is a rich, deep color. Add vinegar and season with salt and pepper to taste. Serve with rice and sprinkle with chopped onion. Makes 4 servings.

BLACK-EYED PEAS WITH MARJORAM

These are delicious with steamed greens, rice, and cornbread.

1½ cups dried black-eyed peas, rinsed and picked over
3 cups water
1 medium onion, chopped (½ cup)
3 tablespoons oil
2 cloves garlic, minced
1 dried red pepper pod or ¼ teaspoon crushed red pepper
1 bay leaf
1 teaspoon marjoram
salt
about 1 tablespoon vinegar, to taste

In saucepan, mix well peas, water, onion, oil, garlic, pepper, bay leaf, and marjoram; bring to boil. Reduce heat, cover, and simmer 45 minutes or until peas are tender. Discard bay leaf. Season to taste with salt and vinegar. Makes 4 servings.

MINNEHAHA BEANS

2 cups dried navy beans, rinsed and picked over
½ cup butter or margarine
1 small onion, minced
½ cup brown sugar, packed
2 tablespoons mild molasses
1 teaspoon salt
½ teaspoon dry mustard

Soak beans as explained on page 129. Drain, reserving liquid. In heavy saucepan, mix well beans, butter, onion, sugar, molasses, salt, and mustard. Add enough reserved liquid barely to cover beans. Cover tightly and simmer 2 hours or until beans are tender. For drier beans and thicker sauce, bake, uncovered, in preheated 400° oven until most of the liquid is absorbed. Makes 6 servings.

ZUCCHINI, HOMINY, AND CHICKPEA CASSEROLE

2 tablespoons flour
2 teaspoons chili powder
1 teaspoon salt
2 medium zucchini, sliced
2 medium tomatoes, sliced
1 large onion, thinly sliced
1 medium green pepper, cut in strips
1 can (16 ounces) hominy, drained
1 can (16 ounces) chickpeas, drained
1 cup shredded Cheddar cheese

Mix flour, chili powder, and salt; set aside. In greased 3-quart casserole, layer half the zucchini, tomatoes, onion, green pepper, hominy, chickpeas, flour mixture, and cheese. Repeat. Cover and bake in preheated 350° oven 1¼ hours or until tender. Makes 6 servings.

TOMATO-CHEESE SOYBEANS

1 cup dried soybeans
salt
vinegar
2 cups cooked corn
1 can (1 pound) tomatoes
1 teaspoon sugar
pepper
1 cup soft bread crumbs
¼ cup butter or margarine, melted
½ cup shredded Cheddar cheese
paprika

Wash beans and soak overnight or by the short-soak method (see page 129). Bring back to the boil and simmer, covered, until nearly tender, 1½ to 2 hours. Drain and season to taste with salt and vinegar. Arrange in alternate layers with corn in shallow 2-quart baking dish. Mix tomatoes, sugar, 1 teaspoon salt, and pepper to taste and pour over mixture. Top with crumbs, drizzle butter over top, and sprinkle with cheese and paprika. Bake, uncovered, in preheated 375° oven about 30 minutes. Makes 6 servings.

CORIANDER LENTILS WITH RIBBON NOODLES

This dish is from the Near East, where coriander is often used to flavor lentils. It is very good with spinach salad on the side.

    1 cup red or brown lentils (see note)
    ¼ cup oil, preferably olive oil
    1 onion, chopped
    2 cloves garlic, minced
    1 tablespoon coriander
    salt
    lemon juice
    1 package (8 ounces) thin egg noodles, cooked *al dente* and
        drained

Rinse and pick over the lentils and put in a pot with about 3 cups of water. Bring to the boil, cover, and simmer until tender but not mushy, anywhere from 30 to 45 minutes. Meanwhile, heat the oil and gently cook the onion and garlic until soft; add coriander and cook for 1 minute. Drain the lentils and stir in the onion mixture; add salt and lemon juice to taste. Mix with noodles and serve immediately. Makes 4 servings.

Note: Red lentils are available in health-food stores and specialty food shops. They cook a bit faster than the brown ones, look prettier, and have more zing.

Pasta

The day has come for pasta-and-vegetable combinations. Match-making is a simple matter: take one of the scores of pasta shapes (smaller, thinner kinds are generally best for this kind of dish), then pick one or more vegetables to go with it. Prepare each, put them together in a light cream or oil sauce, and perhaps sprinkle with cheese. It's a marriage made in heaven.

TIPS FOR PERFECT PASTA

• Use a big pot. Bring water to rapid boil — at least 2 quarts for every 4 ounces of pasta. Add 1 tablespoon salt. If desired, add about 1 teaspoon oil to prevent water from foaming over and pasta from sticking together.

• Add pasta gradually so that water does not stop boiling and, to keep pasta moving, stir with wooden spoon if necessary. (It is not necessary to break long spaghetti in half. Grasp one end of bundle and plunge opposite end in boiling water. As spaghetti softens, push more into water until all is covered; stir to separate.)

• Boil pasta uncovered, stirring occasionally, 8 to 10 minutes for packaged pasta, less for fresh or homemade. Do not overcook. Test a strand or two toward end of cooking. Pasta is more flavorful *al dente* — tender, yet slightly resistant to the bite. (If pasta is to be cooked further in casserole or sauce, reduce boiling time about 2 minutes.)

• Drain at once in colander, shaking colander. Do not rinse. If pasta starts to stick, gently lift and separate strands with fork. Or add a little oil and toss gently. Serve at once with desired sauce.

• If pasta is to be used in a cold salad, rinse with cold water to stop cooking; drain well. If desired, add dressing while pasta is slightly warm to prevent sticking and to blend flavors. Refrigerate.

PASTA PRIMAVERA

Here is a subtle pasta dish that you can make any time of the year at all — winter, summer, or fall, as well as spring. Choose a variety of fresh vegetables according to what looks good in the garden or market.

> about 4 cups mixed in-season vegetables, such as asparagus, peas, green beans, cauliflower, or broccoli
> salt
> ¼ pound mushrooms, sliced
> 1 tablespoon minced parsley
> ½ teaspoon dried basil or 3 fresh basil leaves, minced
> dash of nutmeg
> 10 tablespoons butter or margarine
> 1 pound pasta (ribbon noodles, thin spaghetti, small shells, or other pasta)
> ½ cup heavy cream
> ½ cup grated Parmesan cheese
> pepper

Cook vegetables in boiling salted water until barely tender; drain and rinse under cold water. Cool, then cut in bite-sized pieces and set aside. In large skillet, cook mushrooms, parsley, basil, and nutmeg in 4 tablespoons butter for 5 minutes. Add vegetable mixture; cook 5 minutes longer, stirring. In large kettle, cook pasta *al dente*; drain. In same kettle, melt remaining butter, add pasta, and toss well to coat. Add vegetable mixture and cream; toss well. Serve at once on large warm platter; sprinkle with Parmesan cheese and pepper to taste. Makes 6 servings.

LASAGNA WITH CREAMED MUSHROOMS

Have a white lasagna instead of the more familiar red and serve it with a romaine or watercress and cherry tomato salad. Tart apples and walnuts will round out the meal perfectly.

 3 tablespoons butter or margarine
 1 pound mushrooms, sliced
 3 tablespoons flour
 1 teaspoon salt
 pinch of nutmeg
 2½ cups milk
 3 tablespoons minced parsley
 1 pound ricotta or creamed cottage cheese
 ½ cup grated Parmesan cheese
 9 lasagna strips, cooked *al dente*, drained, and rinsed
 8 ounces mozzarella cheese, coarsely shredded

Melt butter in 3-quart saucepan and sauté mushrooms until wilted, about 6 minutes. Stir in flour, salt, and nutmeg. Gradually blend in milk and cook, stirring constantly, until thickened. Stir in parsley and taste for seasoning. Mix in the ricotta or cottage cheese and half the Parmesan. Cover the bottom of a greased lasagna pan (about 13 x 9 x 2 inches) with three strips of lasagna. Spread a third of the mushroom mixture over them and top with a third of the mozzarella. Repeat twice. Sprinkle with remaining Parmesan and bake in a preheated 375° oven for 30 minutes, or until brown and bubbly. Let stand 10 minutes before cutting. Makes 6 servings.

VEGETABLES WITH SPINACH NOODLES AND COTTAGE CHEESE

 1 cup thinly sliced carrots (about 4)
 1 medium onion, chopped
 2 tablespoons butter or margarine
 ¼ pound mushrooms, sliced
 1 package (8 ounces) spinach noodles, cooked and drained

2 cups cottage cheese (1 pound)
½ cup milk
½ teaspoon basil
½ teaspoon salt
¼ teaspoon thyme
⅛ teaspoon pepper
2 tablespoons grated Parmesan cheese

Cook carrots and onion in butter in large skillet until tender, about 10 minutes. Add mushrooms; cook 5 minutes; set aside. In large bowl, combine remaining ingredients except Parmesan. Stir in vegetables. Turn into greased 2-quart casserole. Cover and bake in preheated 350° oven 30 minutes or until bubbly. Sprinkle with Parmesan. Makes 4 servings.

MANICOTTI STUFFED WITH CHEESE AND VEGETABLES

1 small onion, chopped (¼ cup)
¼ pound fresh mushrooms, chopped
2 tablespoons butter or margarine
16 ounces ricotta or creamed cottage cheese
8 ounces mozzarella cheese, coarsely shredded
2 eggs, beaten
1 teaspoon salt
½ teaspoon nutmeg
pepper
2 packages (10 ounces each) frozen chopped broccoli, cooked and well drained
8 ounces manicotti noodles, cooked *al dente*, drained, and rinsed
Parmesan sauce (see recipe below)
grated Parmesan cheese

In skillet, sauté onion and mushrooms in butter until tender and golden brown. Mix with ricotta or cottage cheese, mozzarella, eggs, salt, nutmeg, and pepper to taste. Stir in broccoli. Using teaspoon or small spatula, fill noodles with cheese mixture. Arrange in two lightly greased 12 x 8 x 2-inch baking dishes or in one large pan. Pour on sauce, then sprinkle with Parmesan. Cover with foil; bake in preheated 350° oven 15 minutes. Uncover and bake 20 minutes longer, or until lightly browned and bubbly. Makes 6 servings.

Parmesan Sauce

Melt ¼ cup butter or margarine in saucepan. Blend in ¼ cup flour and 1 teaspoon salt. Gradually stir in 3 cups milk; stir over medium heat until thick and smooth. Stir in ⅓ cup grated Parmesan. Makes 3 cups.

VARIATION

You may substitute two packages (10 ounces each) frozen chopped spinach, thawed and well drained, for the broccoli.

Dumplings

Try some light and fluffy dumplings for a unique kind of meatless meal. With soup first and a salad on the side, they can be quite substantial.

SPINACH DUMPLINGS

    1 package (10 ounces) frozen chopped spinach, thawed and
        squeezed dry
    2 eggs
    1 cup dry bread crumbs
    1½ cups cottage cheese
    ⅓ cup grated Parmesan or Romano cheese
    2 green onions with tops, finely chopped
    1 clove garlic, finely minced
    1 teaspoon basil
    salt
    2 to 3 tablespoons flour
    about 1½ cups hot spaghetti sauce

Mix well spinach, eggs, bread crumbs, cheeses, onions, garlic, basil, and ½ teaspoon salt. Using rounded tablespoonfuls, shape in balls. Roll in flour. In large saucepan, bring to boil 2 inches salted water. Add half the balls (they'll sink to bottom). Reduce heat; simmer 3 to 4 minutes or until balls float to surface. With slotted spoon, remove to warm dish. Cook remaining balls. Top with sauce. Makes 4 servings.

Note: If desired, balls can be formed and floured up to 2 days ahead. Store covered in refrigerator. Cook just before serving.

GNOCCHI

Certain three-star restaurants charge a fortune for these Italian potato dumplings, which you can easily make at home.

1 pound all-purpose potatoes, peeled
salt
about 1 cup unsifted all-purpose flour
butter or margarine
1 egg, beaten with 1 egg yolk
dash of nutmeg
1 cup grated Parmesan cheese

Boil potatoes in lightly salted water until tender. Drain and dry over low heat a few seconds. Sprinkle board generously with some of the flour. Rice or mash potatoes onto board. With fingers or a fork, quickly work in 2 tablespoons butter, the eggs, about ¾ cup flour, 1 teaspoon salt, and the nutmeg. Gather up mixture and knead lightly with remaining flour and ½ cup cheese, only until dough is smooth and pliable. Cut off egg-sized knobs of dough and roll into long finger-sized rolls. Cut in 1-inch pieces. With back of floured fork, gently roll each piece backward, then press in lightly as you roll it forward to give the characteristic shell-like indentation. Dry on towel 1 hour. Bring large kettle of salted water to boil; drop in some of the gnocchi (leave them plenty of floating room). Cook gently 5 to 6 minutes, or until light and slightly puffed. Remove with strainer or slotted spoon and drop into well-buttered shallow baking dish. Keep warm until all are cooked. Pour ⅓ cup melted butter over top and sprinkle with remaining cheese. Put under broiler a few minutes to glaze lightly. Makes 4 servings.

Note: Gnocchi may also be served with marinara or pesto sauce or gratinéed the French way in a white sauce with cheese (sauce Mornay).

Omelets

The French omelet may well be the last word in elegant simplicity. Golden brown and feathery light, it is the ideal dish for brunch or midnight suppers, or for anytime in between. There is a knack to it, but one that is easy enough to master and well worth the effort.

Success with an omelet depends primarily on the choice of pan. Special omelet pans are available, or use a medium-weight 9- or 10-inch skillet with sloping sides, flat bottom, and smooth surface. Pans with nonstick coating are especially good. (If omelet sticks to pan you are using, see note below.) Give the recipe your undivided attention.

BASIC OMELET

4 large eggs
1 tablespoon cold water
¼ teaspoon salt
dash of pepper
2 tablespoons butter or margarine

Take eggs from refrigerator and break into medium bowl. Add the water, salt, and pepper. With fork, beat eggs briskly 25 to 30 seconds, or just enough to blend yolks and whites. Melt butter in pan over moderate heat until it begins to sizzle and foam (do not brown). Pour in eggs. Hold handle of pan in left hand and fork in right (or the reverse if you are left-handed). As edges of omelet crinkle and look firm, lift toward center with fork so that uncooked egg runs under firm portion. Tilt pan as necessary with left hand to hasten flow of egg. Continue lifting egg with fork until all uncooked egg has run under cooked portion. Smooth top of omelet with fork. Edges should look firm; top, moist and creamy. Entire cooking time will be 3 to 4 minutes. With spatula, lift edge of omelet; if not brown enough, increase heat slightly.

If you are filling the omelet, spread filling across the middle, perpendicular to pan handle. With spatula, fold the third of the omelet nearest the handle toward center. Slide unfolded third of omelet onto center of serving plate. Invert pan, folding omelet over. Serve at once. Makes 2 servings.

Note: To season pan, cover bottom with vegetable oil and heat slowly, turning pan occasionally to coat sides. When hot, remove from heat and cool; let stand overnight. Next day, heat again, pour off oil, and wipe pan dry with paper towel.

VARIATIONS

Herbed Omelet

Add about 1 tablespoon finely chopped fresh herbs to the eggs before cooking. Parsley, chives, chervil, tarragon, and basil, individually or in combination, are good for this purpose.

Spinach Omelet

Fill omelet with about ½ cup hot creamed spinach. Serve with sour cream, if desired.

Vegetable Omelet

Heat small amount of diced cooked vegetables in about 1 tablespoon cream. Fill omelet.

Avocado Omelet

Fill omelet with ½ cup diced avocado seasoned with lemon juice, salt, and pepper. Add 1 or 2 slices of tomato and a sprinkling of alfalfa sprouts. Serve with additional avocado and yogurt, if desired.

Mushroom Omelet

Sauté ¼ pound mushrooms, sliced, in 2 tablespoons butter. Season with salt and pepper. Put some in center of omelet, remainder around sides.

PIPÉRADE OMELET

This is an open-faced omelet made with pipérade, the classic Basque dish of onions, peppers, and tomatoes. The pipérade itself can be made in advance and refrigerated or even frozen; you may also serve it with rice or as a side dish.

    1 medium onion, thinly sliced
    1 clove garlic, crushed
    1 each medium sweet red and green peppers or 2 green peppers,
        cut in ¼-inch strips
    1 tablespoon oil, preferably olive oil
    1 can (16 ounces) tomatoes
    1 teaspoon minced fresh basil, or ¼ teaspoon dried basil
    ⅛ teaspoon black pepper
    4 eggs, slightly beaten with 1 teaspoon salt

In skillet, sauté onion, garlic, and peppers in oil until tender. Add tomatoes, basil, and black pepper, cover and simmer 15 to 25 minutes, or until most of liquid evaporates. Pour in eggs; cook and stir lightly until set. Serve at once. Makes 4 servings.

FRITTATA

An Italian kind of omelet, frittata is also excellent as a first course or one element in an antipasto.

    1 clove garlic, halved
    2 tablespoons oil
    1 pound zucchini, cut in ½-inch slices
    1 onion, quartered and sliced
    8 to 10 eggs, lightly beaten
    2 tablespoons grated Parmesan cheese

In large skillet, sauté garlic in oil until lightly browned; discard. Add zucchini and onion and stir until coated with oil; cover and cook over low heat, stirring once or twice, about 5 minutes, or until zucchini is tender. Spread the zucchini and onion evenly in the skillet and add eggs. Turn heat very low, cover pan, and cook until eggs are set. Sprinkle with cheese and brown top under broiler. Cut in wedges. Serve hot or at room temperature. Makes 4 servings as a main dish, 8 as an appetizer.

Soufflés

Rumor has it that it takes a genius to make a soufflé. This is positively not true. Anyone can succeed in making a beautiful, puffy, delectable soufflé every time by faithfully following a few basic rules. This is a dish that can and should be in every cook's repertoire.

TIPS FOR PERFECT SOUFFLES

• Remove the eggs from the refrigerator, separate them, and let them stand for at least 1 hour before starting the soufflé. You do this because eggs are easiest to separate when cold, but you can beat the whites to greater volume at room temperature.

• Make sure the whites go into a perfectly clean, dry bowl. The tiniest bit of grease, moisture, or egg yolk will keep the whites from mounting properly. If any yolk gets into the white, scoop it out with a piece of eggshell.

• Beat the whites until they are shiny and stiff enough to hold a good peak when lifted on the beater. Do not beat after this point. Use a wire whisk, rotary eggbeater, or electric mixer, working so as to incorporate as much air as possible into the whites. Do not hesitate to use cream of tartar to help the whites to mount and hold the air.

• Fold the egg whites carefully into the soufflé base. First mix some whites into the base to lighten it, then fold in the rest.

• Bake the soufflé in a dish with straight sides and a flat bottom. This classic shape is available in china, glass, and metal and in sizes from 1 to 8 cups. Use the right-sized dish. If you do not have one the right size, use one that is smaller rather than larger and fashion a two- or three-inch collar around it. Aluminum foil, folded over once or twice and held together with straight pins or paper clips, is ideal, but you can also use waxed paper or brown paper, folded over and held in place with string. Be sure to butter the collar when you butter the dish.

• Keep the oven door closed during baking to keep the soufflé from falling. If you cannot resist a peek, do it after the first 25 minutes and make it fast.

• Have everything — and everybody — ready so that you can serve the soufflé immediately.

BASIC SOUFFLE

4 eggs
3 tablespoons butter
3 tablespoons flour
1 cup milk
salt and pepper
¼ teaspoon cream of tartar

Separate the eggs. Melt butter in a heavy saucepan and stir in flour. Cook for 1 or 2 minutes, then gradually add milk. Simmer, stirring constantly, until thickened. (Add cheese and vegetables, if any, at this point.) Season to taste with salt and pepper and beat in the egg yolks one at a time. Beat the egg whites until frothy, add the cream of tartar, and continue beating until whites are stiff and shiny. Mix some beaten whites into the yolk mixture, then carefully fold in the rest. Turn into a greased 6-cup soufflé mold and bake in a preheated 375° oven 15 minutes; reduce heat to 350° and continue baking 30 minutes or until soufflé is puffed and golden brown. Makes 3 servings as a main dish, 6 servings as a side dish.

VARIATIONS

Cheese Soufflé on Broiled Tomatoes
Peel 4 large tomatoes and cut each in 4 slices. Season with salt and pepper and broil 1 minute on each side. Transfer to rounds

of buttered toast and arrange in long shallow baking pan. Make soufflé, adding 1 cup shredded Cheddar cheese after milk thickens; cook until it melts. Proceed with recipe, but instead of pouring the soufflé mixture into a dish, heap it on tomato slices. Bake in preheated 400° oven for 15 minutes or until puffed and golden brown. Garnish with watercress.

Spinach or Kale Soufflé

Sauté 1 small minced onion in 1 tablespoon butter until tender. Add 1 package (10 ounces) frozen spinach or kale, thawed and drained. Cook and stir to evaporate any liquid; season to taste with cayenne pepper and nutmeg, if desired, and set aside. Before adding egg yolks to soufflé base, stir in 1 cup shredded Swiss cheese and cook until melted. Add spinach or kale mixture and proceed with master recipe.

Asparagus Soufflé

Just before adding yolks, season to taste with nutmeg and stir in 3 tablespoons grated Parmesan cheese. Add 1 cup chopped cooked asparagus and continue with recipe.

Broccoli-Onion Soufflé

When milk has thickened, add 1 tablespoon lemon juice, 2 tablespoons grated onion, and 1 cup finely chopped cooked broccoli. Proceed with master recipe.

Eggplant Soufflé

Peel and dice 1 large eggplant. Cook in small amount of boiling water until tender, drain well, and rub through a coarse sieve. Before adding egg yolks, stir in ½ cup grated Parmesan cheese, 1 tablespoon catsup, 1 teaspoon grated onion, and the mashed eggplant. Continue with recipe.

DOUBLE CORN SOUFFLE

This is really a cross between a soufflé and a corn pudding. Note how well the curry complements the corn and carrot.

  2 tablespoons butter or margarine
  1 tablespoon flour
  1 teaspoon salt
  ⅛ teaspoon pepper
  1 teaspoon curry powder, or more to taste
  1 can (16 or 17 ounces) cream-style corn
  1 cup whole kernel corn, cooked or canned
  4 eggs, separated
  1 carrot, peeled and shredded
  1 cup sour cream
  2 tablespoons fine dry bread crumbs

Melt butter and blend in flour and seasonings. Stir in corn, beaten egg yolks, carrot, and sour cream. Taste for seasoning. Fold in stiffly beaten egg whites and pour into shallow buttered 1½-quart baking dish. Sprinkle with crumbs. Bake in preheated 350° oven about 35 minutes. Makes 4 servings as a main dish, 6 servings as a side dish.

Quiches

The quiche, once considered fancy fare, has been adopted by American cooks. Its popularity is not hard to understand: a quiche is always delicious, usually inexpensive, and quite easy to prepare.

Basically, a quiche is a savory custard baked in a pastry shell. Nothing could be simpler. At home in Belgium and France, where it originated, the shell is free-standing; in bistros, the quiche is more often prepared in a rectangular pan like a cookie sheet. Quiche pans that are attractive enough to bring to the table are also available. On the other hand, an excellent quiche in a plain old pie tin is nothing to be ashamed of. For the custard, consult each recipe; for the shell, prepare a short pastry or American-style pie crust — whatever works best for you.

ASPARAGUS QUICHE

    9-inch pastry shell
    2 cups cooked asparagus, cut in 1-inch pieces
    1 cup shredded Gruyère or Swiss cheese
    1 cup light cream
    3 eggs, slightly beaten
    1 teaspoon dried tarragon, or 1 tablespoon minced fresh tarragon
    ¼ teaspoon nutmeg
    ½ teaspoon salt
    dash of pepper

Prick pastry shell with fork and bake in preheated 450° oven 7 minutes; cool. Put asparagus, then cheese, in shell. In bowl, mix well cream, eggs, and seasonings. Pour gently over cheese. Bake in preheated 350° oven 30 minutes, or until set and puffy. Makes 4 to 6 servings.

VARIATIONS

For a heartier version, add 8 slices of bacon, cooked and crumbled, or 1 cup diced cooked ham with the asparagus.

Broccoli Quiche
Substitute 2 cups cooked, chopped broccoli for the asparagus. Use either Swiss or Cheddar cheese.

TARTE À L'OIGNON

Make a meal of this onion quiche with soup and a salad, or serve it as an appetizer with an unpretentious white wine as they do in Alsace, its native land.

>   9-inch pastry shell
>   2 large sweet onions (about 1½ pounds)
>   ⅓ cup butter
>   1 tablespoon flour
>   3 eggs, slightly beaten
>   1 cup light cream
>   salt and pepper
>   nutmeg
>   ½ cup grated Romano cheese

Prick pastry shell with fork and bake in preheated 450° oven 7 minutes; cool. Meanwhile, cut onions in quarters and slice ¼-inch thick. Sauté in butter until soft and light yellow, about 8 to 10 minutes, stirring occasionally. Blend in flour, eggs, and cream; season to taste with salt, pepper, and nutmeg. Pour into pastry shell, sprinkle with cheese. Bake in preheated 350° oven 30 to 35 minutes, or until set. May be served hot or at room temperature. Makes 4 servings as a main dish, 6 or more as an appetizer or side dish.

ZUCCHINI-PEPPER PIE

9-inch pastry shell
3 medium zucchini (1 pound), thinly sliced
2 green onions with tops, sliced
1 large clove garlic, minced
2 tablespoons oil
1 medium tomato, peeled and chopped
1 medium green pepper, chopped
¾ teaspoon salt
½ teaspoon basil
¼ teaspoon pepper
3 eggs
½ cup heavy cream
¼ cup grated Parmesan cheese

Prick bottom of pie shell and bake in preheated 450° oven 7 minutes or until lightly browned. Cool. Sauté zucchini, onions, and garlic in oil about 5 minutes, stirring occasionally. Stir in tomato, green pepper, salt, basil, and pepper. Cook over low heat, stirring occasionally, until vegetables are tender and liquid has evaporated, about 10 minutes. Spread vegetables evenly in shell. Beat eggs and cream until mixed; pour over vegetables. Sprinkle with Parmesan. Bake in 350° oven 30 minutes, or until set. Makes 4 to 6 servings.

SPINACH QUICHE WITH RICOTTA CHEESE

9-inch pastry shell
1 tablespoon minced onion or green onion
1 tablespoon butter
1 package (10 ounces) frozen chopped spinach, thawed and
    drained
salt and pepper
nutmeg
½ cup ricotta or small-curd cottage cheese
3 eggs
½ cup heavy cream
¼ cup coarsely grated Swiss cheese

Prick pastry shell with fork and bake in preheated 450° oven 7 minutes; cool. Sauté onions in butter. Add spinach and stir over moderate heat to evaporate all liquid. Season to taste with salt, pepper, and nutmeg. Stir in ricotta. Beat eggs and cream together and stir into spinach mixture. Add the cheese and pour into shell. Bake in preheated 350° oven 30 to 35 minutes, or until set. Makes 4 to 6 servings.

Main-Dish Salads

What could be more refreshing than a cold salad on a hot day? Try one of these meatless combinations the next time the temperature soars.

SPRING RICE SALAD

    3 cups cooked rice, cooled
    1⅓ cups cooked dried beans
    1 cup finely diced celery (3 large ribs)
    2 hard-cooked eggs, chopped
    ¼ cup chopped green pepper
    ¼ cup sliced pimiento-stuffed green olives
    ¼ cup sliced green onion
    2 tablespoons diced radishes
    ½ cup mayonnaise
    1 tablespoon lemon juice
    ½ teaspoon salt, or to taste
    lettuce leaves
    minced parsley for garnish

In large bowl, combine all ingredients except lettuce and parsley. Cover and refrigerate 4 to 6 hours to blend flavors. To serve, line a bowl with lettuce leaves, add salad, and sprinkle with parsley. Makes 4 servings as a main dish, 8 servings as a side dish.

TABBOULEH

This salad of bulgur, garden vegetables, and legumes, topped off with a refreshing dollop of mint-flavored yogurt, has long been a

hot-weather favorite in the Middle East. Create your own vegetable combination or follow the suggestions below. For an individual portion, start with ¼ cup of bulgur.

2 cups bulgur (see note)
1 to 1½ cups chickpeas, cooked or canned
1 cup shredded carrots
1 cup cooked green beans
2 tomatoes, seeded and chopped
¼ pound mushrooms, sliced
⅓ cup sliced green onion
¼ cup minced parsley
¼ cup each lemon juice and oil
1¼ teaspoons salt
¼ teaspoon pepper
lettuce leaves
tomato slices
2 cups yogurt mixed with 2 tablespoons chopped fresh mint, or 2
    teaspoons dried mint

In large bowl, soak bulgur in cold water to cover, 45 minutes;
drain well. Add chickpeas, carrots, green beans, tomatoes, mushrooms, onions, parsley, lemon juice, oil, salt, and pepper; toss to
mix. Chill at least 1 hour. Turn out in lettuce-lined salad bowl.
Garnish with tomato slices. Spoon on mint-yogurt dressing. Makes
8 servings.

Note: Bulgur (cracked wheat) is available in health-food stores,
in specialty food shops, and on the ethnic or gourmet foods shelf
of some supermarkets.

GADO GADO

Hot peppers in a peanut sauce make this salad from Indonesia
good and hot!

3 carrots, peeled and cut in matchsticks
½ pound fresh green beans, cut in thin diagonals
salt

4 cups shredded salad greens (lettuce, spinach, escarole, or
    chicory)
3 medium potatoes, cooked, peeled, diced, and cooled
about 1 cup bean sprouts, rinsed and drained
1 tomato, cut in wedges
3 hard-cooked eggs, quartered
peanut sauce (see recipe below)

Steam carrots and beans separately in small amounts of salted
water until crisp-tender; drain, reserving liquid for peanut sauce.
Chill vegetables. Spread greens on large platter. Arrange carrots,
potatoes, green beans, and bean sprouts on top. Garnish with tomato wedges and egg quarters. Chill until serving time. Serve
with peanut sauce. Makes 6 servings.

Peanut Sauce

    ¼ cup minced onion
    1 tablespoon butter or margarine
    1 cup water (including water drained from vegetables)
    ½ cup peanut butter
    1 tablespoon lemon juice
    ½ teaspoon salt
    ¼ to ½ teaspoon crushed dried red peppers

Sauté onion in butter until tender. Add water and peanut butter,
stirring until smooth. Add remaining ingredients; chill.

VEGETABLE AND BROWN RICE SALAD

    3 cups cooked brown rice, cooled
    1⅓ cups cooked dried beans
    ¾ cup coarsely shredded carrot
    ¾ cup coarsely shredded zucchini
    3 tablespoons chopped parsley (see note)
    2 tablespoons sliced green onion
    2 tablespoons lemon juice
    1 tablespoon oil
    ½ teaspoon salt, or to taste

In large bowl, mix all ingredients. Refrigerate several hours or overnight. Makes 4 servings as a main dish, 8 servings as a side dish.

Note: Fresh herbs are essential here. When you have them, use chopped oregano or marjoram, tarragon, or basil, alone or in combination, in place of the parsley, which is available year round.

6

MAIN DISHES WITH FISH, CHICKEN, OR MEAT

Throughout the rest of this book, vegetables have been treated separately from meat or fish, as soups or salads or side dishes. In this chapter, these ingredients are back together again. Here are the stews, casseroles, and salads that are the cook's salvation, the dishes that can be assembled in advance and set aside until it is time to put them on to simmer or bake. These are one-pot meals to please family and guests alike.

Many of the recipes are time-tested classics; only a few are of recent origin. That spicy lamb and eggplant casserole, moussaka, for example, was spread to Europe by the Ottoman Turks centuries ago, along with the tomato and the green pepper. Brunswick stew, with chicken, okra, and lima beans, is an old American crowd-pleaser.

One thing is certain: almost any vegetable can go into the stew pot with meat. Chunks of sweet potato and corn on the cob are stewed with beef in our Mexican vegetable stew; Italian green beans go with veal in another recipe. Layered casseroles, such as cabbage meat loaf or zucchini-hamburger casserole, use a variety of vegetables in combination with shredded or ground meat.

In this kind of recipe, you can make changes — increase or decrease the amount of meat, substitute other spices, use different vegetables. Moussaka, for example, is often made with potatoes when eggplant is out of season. The cabbage and summer squash families, as well as eggplant and potatoes, are very well suited to layering. Vegetables that hold their shape when cooked are good to add to stews. The key thing is to get nature's bounty on the table and sit down and enjoy it!

Fish and Shellfish

BAKED FISH FILLETS WITH CUCUMBER AND GREEN PEPPER STUFFING

2 medium green peppers, seeded and cut in ¾-inch strips (chop
  enough to make ½ cup)
2 cups soft bread crumbs
1 medium cucumber, peeled, seeded, and diced (about ¾ cup)
3 tablespoons butter or margarine, melted
2 tablespoons water
2 tablespoons grated onion
2 tablespoons minced parsley
½ teaspoon salt
¼ teaspoon thyme
¼ teaspoon grated lemon peel
3 teaspoons lemon juice
⅛ teaspoon pepper
4 flounder fillets (about 1 pound), thawed if frozen
2 teaspoons Dijon mustard
2 teaspoons Worcestershire sauce
4 teaspoons chili sauce or catsup

Mix together chopped green pepper, bread crumbs, cucumber, butter, water, onion, parsley, salt, thyme, lemon peel, 1 teaspoon lemon juice, and pepper. Place packed ½ cup stuffing on center of each fish fillet. Bring ends of fish over stuffing, overlapping; fasten with wooden pick. Place fish bundles side by side in greased 12 x 8 x 2-inch baking dish. Bake in preheated 350° oven 20 minutes. Meanwhile, mix well remaining 2 teaspoons lemon juice, the mustard, Worcestershire sauce, and chili sauce or catsup. Arrange green pepper strips on fish; brush all with mustard sauce. Bake 10 minutes, or until fish flakes easily with fork. Makes 4 servings.

SALADE NIÇOISE

6 new potatoes, cooked, peeled, and diced
herbed vinaigrette dressing (see recipe below)
2 cups green beans, cooked and cooled
1 head romaine lettuce
2 tomatoes, cut in wedges
1 hard-cooked egg, quartered
12 oil-cured black olives
1 can (7 ounces) tuna, drained
1 small green pepper, seeded and thinly sliced in rings
1 medium red onion, thinly sliced
1 can (2 ounces) anchovy fillets, drained

Toss potatoes with about 1 tablespoon dressing; cover and chill. Toss beans with 1 tablespoon dressing; cover and chill. Arrange lettuce on large platter or in shallow salad bowl. Mound potatoes in center, then arrange beans, tomatoes, egg, olives, tuna, green pepper, onion, and anchovies around them. Pour remaining dressing over all. Bring to table. Toss gently just before serving. Makes 4 servings.

Herbed Vinaigrette Dressing
In small jar, shake to mix well ½ cup olive oil, 1 tablespoon minced parsley, 3 tablespoons red wine vinegar, 1 teaspoon each salt and Dijon mustard, 1 crushed medium clove garlic, ⅛ teaspoon pepper, and, if desired, ¼ teaspoon tarragon. Makes about ¾ cup.

STUFFED CHAYOTE

Chayote, a subtropical squash, may be found in Latin markets. It is deeply ribbed, pear-shaped, and has a greenish-white rind and one seed. If the seed is soft and underdeveloped, it may be cooked and eaten with the squash. If it is hard, discard it. If chayotes are not available, use eggplant or yellow or green summer squash.

2 chayotes (about 1 pound each), split lengthwise
salt
3 tablespoons butter or margarine
1 large onion, minced (1 cup)
1 medium-sized green pepper, chopped (½ cup)
3 large ribs celery, thinly sliced (¾ cup)
1 large clove garlic, or to taste, crushed
6 to 8 ounces small shrimps, cooked, shelled, deveined, and
    chopped (reserve 4 whole shrimps for garnish)
1¼ cups soft bread crumbs
1 large bay leaf, crumbled (½ teaspoon)
¼ teaspoon hot pepper sauce, or to taste
1 tablespoon melted butter or margarine

Place chayotes (with soft seeds if present) in large skillet in about 1 inch boiling salted water; cover and cook until tender, 25 to 30 minutes, turning once or twice. Drain cut side down on paper towels; scoop out flesh and seeds, leaving thick shells. Cut flesh and seeds in small pieces; set aside. Melt butter in skillet or saucepan; sauté until tender onion, green pepper, celery, and garlic, stirring often. Stir in chayote flesh and seeds, shrimps, 1 cup bread crumbs, 1 teaspoon salt, bay leaf, and pepper sauce; mix well. Fill chayote shells. Mix remaining crumbs with melted butter and sprinkle on top. Bake in shallow baking pan in 375° oven 25 to 30 minutes, or until hot and crumbs are lightly browned. Makes 4 servings.

MUSHROOM-TUNA CASSEROLE

½ pound mushrooms
4 tablespoons butter or margarine
½ cup diced celery
¼ cup chopped onion
2 tablespoons flour
2 cups milk
1 teaspoon salt
dash of cayenne
¼ teaspoon dry mustard

1 can (9¼ ounces) tuna
2 cups cooked rice
¼ cup slivered almonds (optional)
½ cup shredded Cheddar cheese
⅓ cup cracker crumbs

Remove mushroom stems and chop; slice caps. In 2 tablespoons butter, sauté lightly celery, onion, mushroom caps, and stems. Blend in flour and gradually stir in milk. Add seasonings and cook, stirring, until thickened. Drain and flake tuna; combine with rice, almonds if desired, and cheese, reserving 2 tablespoons cheese to sprinkle on top. Add sauce and toss lightly to mix. Turn into 2-quart casserole. Melt remaining butter and mix with cracker crumbs. Sprinkle crumbs and remaining cheese on top. Bake in preheated 375° oven about 30 minutes. Makes 6 servings.

FISH-VEGETABLE SALAD

2 green peppers, cut in 1-inch chunks
2 ribs celery, cut in ½-inch slices
3 green onions, cut in ½-inch pieces
1 carrot, thinly sliced
1 zucchini, thinly sliced
½ cup black olives, pitted
⅓ cup oil
2 tablespoons lemon juice, or more to taste
1 teaspoon salt
pepper
1 pound fish fillets, poached, chilled, and flaked
crisp salad greens
2 tomatoes, cut in chunks
chopped parsley

Combine green peppers, celery, green onions, carrot, zucchini, olives, oil, lemon juice, salt, and pepper to taste. Taste: more salt or lemon juice may be needed. Gently stir in fish. Arrange greens on platter and spoon fish mixture in center. Garnish with tomato and parsley. Makes 4 servings.

SALAD SUPPER

5 medium potatoes, peeled
2 tablespoons each minced parsley and green onion
2 tablespoons salad oil
1 tablespoon vinegar
salt and pepper
⅓ cup mayonnaise
½ bunch watercress, coarsely chopped
4 cups shredded salad greens
1 avocado
½ lemon
2 large tomatoes, peeled and cut in wedges
1 cucumber, peeled and cut in spears
1 large green pepper, seeded and sliced in rings
½ red onion, thinly sliced and separated in rings
½ cup oil-cured black olives, pitted
¼ pound feta cheese, diced
½ pound shrimps, cooked, cleaned, and chilled
1 bunch radishes, cleaned
vinaigrette dressing

Cook and dice potatoes and, while still warm, toss with parsley, green onion, oil, vinegar, and salt and pepper to taste; add mayonnaise. Chill until ready to serve. Arrange bed of watercress and greens on large platter. Halve the avocado, remove pit, peel, and cut in wedges. Rub flesh with lemon to prevent darkening. Mound potatoes in center of greens and arrange tomato wedges, avocado, cucumber, green pepper, onion, black olives, and cheese around edge of platter. Border potato mound with shrimps. Garnish with radishes. Serve with dressing. Makes 6 servings.

Chicken

BRUNSWICK STEW

This is an old crowd-pleaser. Follow up with melon for dessert.

1 frying chicken, cut up
2 ounces lean salt pork, diced
1 dried red pepper or ¼ teaspoon crushed dried red pepper
1 clove garlic
1 tablespoon salt
½ teaspoon pepper
1 can (1 pound) tomatoes, cut up
3 medium potatoes, peeled and diced
2 medium onions, chopped
1½ cups fresh okra or 1 package (10 ounces) frozen okra
2 cups fresh lima beans or 1 box (10 ounces) frozen limas
2 cups cooked corn kernels

Put chicken, salt pork, red pepper, garlic, salt, and pepper and 2 quarts water in large kettle, bring to boil, and simmer, covered, 45 minutes to 1 hour, or until chicken is tender. Remove it, discard skin and bones, shred meat, and set aside. Skim broth, add 1 quart water, the tomatoes, and juice. Bring to boil and add potatoes, onions, okra, and limas. Cover and simmer 25 minutes. Stir in corn and chicken meat and heat through, about 10 minutes. Taste for seasoning and serve. Makes 8 servings.

CHUNKY CHICKEN SALAD

1 tablespoon white wine vinegar
⅓ cup vegetable oil
1 teaspoon salt
¼ teaspoon white pepper
½ teaspoon crushed tarragon leaves
2 cups white chicken or turkey meat, in chunks
1 cup thinly sliced fresh mushrooms
1 small green pepper, thinly sliced
2 medium tomatoes, cut in wedges
1 small cucumber, peeled and sliced
lettuce
1 hard-cooked egg yolk, sieved or finely chopped

Combine vinegar, oil, salt, pepper, and tarragon in large bowl. Add chicken or turkey, mushrooms, and green pepper and toss lightly. Cover and marinate in refrigerator for at least 1 hour. Add tomatoes and cucumber, toss, and pile on lettuce. Sprinkle with egg yolk. Makes 4 servings.

ORIENTAL CHICKEN SALAD

2 whole chicken breasts, boned
soy sauce
4 tablespoons salad oil
1 clove garlic, scored
¾ teaspoon grated lemon rind
4 cups torn spinach leaves
4 cups thinly sliced Chinese cabbage
1 tablespoon lemon juice
salt
2 tablespoons sesame seed, toasted

Cut chicken breasts in strips about ¼ x 2 inches. Marinate several hours in 1 tablespoon soy sauce, 2 tablespoons oil, the garlic, and ½ teaspoon lemon rind. Sauté marinated chicken strips in 1 tablespoon oil until lightly browned, then chill. Just before serving, toss spinach and cabbage with remaining oil, 1 teaspoon soy sauce, remaining lemon rind, lemon juice, and salt to taste until leaves are evenly coated. Add chicken and sesame seed, toss, and serve at once. Makes 6 servings.

SMOTHERED MUSHROOMS AND CHICKEN LIVERS

¾ pound chicken livers
3 tablespoons flour
3 tablespoons butter or margarine
3 tablespoons minced onion
1½ cups sliced mushrooms
salt
dash of pepper
1 cup chicken broth
1 cup uncooked rice
½ cup grated Parmesan cheese
¼ cup port wine
¼ cup heavy cream
2 teaspoons capers (optional)

Sprinkle livers with flour and brown on all sides in the butter. Add onion, mushrooms, ½ teaspoon salt, and pepper. Cook a few minutes, then add broth and simmer 10 minutes. Meanwhile, cook rice, shape in ring in deep platter, and sprinkle with cheese. Add remaining ingredients to livers, heat, and put in center of rice ring. Makes 6 servings.

BROCCOLI AND CHICKEN AU GRATIN

1½ to 2 pounds fresh broccoli or 2 packages (10 ounces each) frozen broccoli spears, thawed
1½ to 2 cups chicken, cut in julienne strips
¼ cup butter or margarine
¼ cup flour
¼ teaspoon salt, or more to taste
2 cups chicken broth
about 1½ cups shredded Cheddar cheese
1 teaspoon Worcestershire sauce

Steam or boil broccoli until almost tender, drain, and arrange in 12 x 8 x 2-inch baking dish. Sprinkle with chicken; set aside. In saucepan, melt butter; blend in flour and salt until smooth and bubbly. Gradually stir in broth. Cook over low heat, stirring constantly, until thickened. Remove from heat and stir in 1 cup cheese and the Worcestershire sauce; stir until cheese melts. Taste for seasoning. Pour over chicken and broccoli. Sprinkle with remaining ½ cup cheese if desired. Bake in preheated 400° oven 20 minutes, or until hot. Makes 4 servings.

Beef

MEXICAN VEGETABLE STEW

Warm cornbread is an excellent partner for this stew; fresh fruit, the perfect dessert.

 1 pound beef stew meat, cut in 1-inch cubes
 2 tablespoons oil
 1 large onion, coarsely chopped
 3 tablespoons chopped canned green chilies
 about ¾ cup beef broth or water
 1 cup diced tomatoes, fresh or canned, drained and peeled
 2 medium cloves garlic, crushed
 1 teaspoon salt
 ½ teaspoon ground cumin
 ¼ teaspoon pepper
 2 medium sweet potatoes, peeled and cut in 1-inch pieces
 2 large ears corn, thawed if frozen, cut in 1-inch pieces
 3 medium zucchini, cut in 1-inch pieces

   In large heavy saucepan or Dutch oven, brown meat evenly in hot oil. Remove; set aside. In same pan, sauté onion and chilies until tender, about 5 minutes. Stir in broth or water, tomatoes, garlic, salt, cumin, and pepper. Add meat, cover, and simmer 1 to 1½ hours, or until meat is almost tender, stirring occasionally. Add sweet potatoes; cover and cook 15 minutes. Add corn, zucchini, and, if necessary, more broth or water (stew should not be too soupy); cover and cook 25 minutes, or until meat and vegetables are tender. Taste for seasoning. Makes 4 servings.

BEEF AND VEGETABLE STIR-FRY

soy sauce
1 tablespoon dry sherry
3 tablespoons oil
1 teaspoon sugar
¼ teaspoon ginger
¾ to 1 pound beef round steak, partially frozen, then thinly sliced
    diagonally
4 large green onions with tops, sliced diagonally
2 cups vegetables (green beans, asparagus, broccoli or zucchini,
    cut in ½-inch slices, or whole snow peas)
3 ounces mushrooms, sliced (about 1 cup)
¾ cup beef broth
steamed rice

In bowl, mix 3 tablespoons soy sauce, sherry, 1 tablespoon oil, sugar, and ginger. Add beef; toss to mix and let stand several minutes. Drain beef, reserving marinade. Heat 2 tablespoons oil in large skillet or wok and stir-fry onions until crisp-tender, about 2 minutes. Push to one side of pan. Add vegetables; stir-fry 2 minutes, then push aside. Add beef a few strips at a time; quickly stir-fry about 30 seconds, then mix in with vegetables. Add mushrooms, reserved marinade, and broth. Heat through and serve over rice; pass soy sauce if desired. Makes 4 servings.

LIVER AND BROCCOLI STIR-FRY

1 tablespoon cornstarch
¼ teaspoon each ginger and pepper
⅓ cup soy sauce
½ pound beef liver, cut in 3 x ½-inch strips
3 tablespoons oil
1 large onion, thinly sliced lengthwise
1 small bunch broccoli, cut in flowerets, or 1 package (10 ounces)
    frozen broccoli spears, partially thawed and cut in 1-inch
    chunks

1 can (8 ounces) water chestnuts, drained and sliced
¼ pound mushrooms, thinly sliced (about 1¼ cups)
1 medium clove garlic, crushed
steamed rice

In bowl, blend cornstarch, ginger, pepper, ½ cup water, and soy sauce. Add liver, mix well, and marinate. Heat oil in large skillet or wok and stir-fry onion, broccoli, chestnuts, mushrooms, and garlic until barely crisp-tender, about 3 minutes. Push to one side of pan. Remove liver from soy-sauce mixture and stir-fry in hot pan until browned, about 2 minutes. Add soy mixture; cook and stir until mixture thickens and comes to boil. Serve with rice. Makes 4 servings.

CABBAGE MEAT LOAF

1 small head cabbage
1 tablespoon oil
1 small onion, chopped
1 tablespoon minced parsley
1½ pounds ground beef
1½ teaspoons salt
½ teaspoon pepper
½ teaspoon ground nutmeg
1 cup fine soft bread crumbs
½ cup beef broth
1 can (8 ounces) tomato sauce
1 tablespoon sugar
1 teaspoon Worcestershire sauce

Quarter and core cabbage. Cook in boiling salted water for 10 minutes; drain. Heat oil and sauté onion until soft; add parsley and cook 1 minute. Mix in with meat, seasonings, bread crumbs, and broth. Arrange in alternate layers with cabbage in greased 9-inch loaf pan, starting and ending with meat. Mix remaining ingredients and pour over top. Bake in preheated 375° oven about 1 hour. Let stand 10 minutes before turning out of pan. Makes 8 servings.

GREEN BEAN AND BEEF SALAD

1 tablespoon mustard, preferably Dijon
1 tablespoon vinegar
¼ cup oil
basil
salt and pepper
2 cups green beans, cooked or canned
1 small onion, thinly sliced
1½ cups cooked steak or roast beef, cut in julienne strips (8
    ounces)
crisp salad greens
sliced tomatoes

In bowl, beat mustard, vinegar, oil, ¼ teaspoon each basil, salt, and pepper until blended. Toss in beans, onion, and beef; marinate at room temperature at least 30 minutes. Serve on greens with tomatoes seasoned with basil, salt, and pepper to taste. Makes 4 servings.

KROPPKAKOR

In the unlikely event there are some of these Swedish dumplings left over, cut them in thirds and fry them in butter until they are crisp and golden.

1 medium onion, minced (⅓ cup)
1 tablespoon butter or margarine
1 cup minced cooked pork, beef, or ham (4 ounces)
¼ teaspoon each allspice and pepper
salt
8 to 10 medium potatoes (2½ pounds), cooked, peeled, and cooled
flour
2 eggs
minced parsley
melted butter to taste

In skillet, sauté onion in butter until tender, about 5 minutes. Add meat and seasonings, including ¼ teaspoon salt. Sauté and stir 2 minutes longer to blend; set aside. In large kettle, bring 4 quarts water with 1 tablespoon salt to boil. Meanwhile, force potatoes through ricer, food mill, or grinder and measure 5 cups into bowl. Add 1 cup flour or enough to make mixture stiff. (To test for correct consistency, break off small piece of dough and drop into boiling water. If dough holds together, proceed as above. If not, add more flour to stiffen.) Add eggs and 1 teaspoon salt; mix until well blended. Turn mixture out onto lightly floured surface and shape into 10-inch log. Cut in 1-inch slices. Make an indentation in center of each slice and fill with meat-onion mixture. With lightly floured hands, shape each into ball, covering filling completely. Flatten dumplings to about 2½-inch patties. Drop one by one into boiling salted water. Bring back to boil over medium heat; simmer, uncovered, 5 minutes after dumplings float to surface. With slotted spoon, remove at once to heated platter. Sprinkle with parsley. Serve hot with melted butter. Makes 4 servings.

ZUCCHINI-HAMBURGER CASSEROLE

4 cups sliced zucchini (about 4 medium)
salt
2 tablespoons oil
1 medium onion, chopped
2 cloves garlic, minced
1 pound ground beef
½ teaspoon oregano
¼ teaspoon pepper
1 cup cooked rice
1 can (8 ounces) tomato sauce
1 cup cottage cheese
¾ cup shredded sharp Cheddar cheese
1 egg

Toss zucchini with 1 teaspoon salt and let stand 20 minutes; drain. Place half in greased 2-quart casserole. Heat oil in skillet and sauté onion and garlic until soft; add meat and cook until completely browned. Skim the fat and add oregano, pepper, and ½ teaspoon salt or more to taste. Stir in rice and tomato sauce. Spread over zucchini in casserole. Mix well cottage cheese, ½ cup Cheddar cheese, and egg; spoon over meat mixture. Top with remaining zucchini and sprinkle with rest of Cheddar. Bake in preheated 350° oven 20 to 25 minutes, or until bubbly. Makes 6 servings.

Veal

VEAL WITH ITALIAN GREEN BEANS

1 pound veal for scallopini
3 tablespoons flour mixed with ¼ teaspoon pepper
3 tablespoons butter or margarine
1 tablespoon oil
2 large onions, sliced
1 package (10 ounces) Italian green beans, partially thawed to
    separate or ¾ pound fresh beans, cut diagonally in ¾-inch
    pieces
1 large clove garlic, crushed
½ cup dry white wine
1 teaspoon salt
lemon wedges (optional)
steamed rice

With flat side of wooden mallet or rolling pin, pound veal very
thin between sheets of waxed paper, being careful not to split
fibers. Coat veal with flour mixture; pound again. Heat butter and
oil in skillet; brown veal a few pieces at a time on both sides, removing pieces as they brown. In drippings, sauté onions, beans,
and garlic until crisp-tender. Add wine, stirring up brown bits.
Add meat and salt. Cover and simmer 5 minutes, or until veal and
vegetables are tender. Garnish with lemon wedges, if desired.
Serve with rice. Makes 6 servings.

VEAL AND MUSHROOM STEW

This dish is good with noodles or rice; serve a cucumber and lettuce salad on the side.

1½ pounds veal stew meat, cut in 1-inch cubes
2 tablespoons oil
1 large onion, finely chopped
1 teaspoon salt
pepper
½ pound mushrooms, sliced
2 tablespoons butter or margarine
1 tablespoon flour
½ cup sour cream
2 tablespoons minced parsley

Brown meat in oil. Add onion and cook 8 to 10 minutes. Add ¾ cup water, salt, and pepper to taste. Bring to boil, cover, and simmer 45 minutes or until meat is tender. Sauté mushrooms in butter and add to veal. Mix flour with sour cream, add a bit of sauce, then carefully blend into stew. Simmer very gently for 5 minutes, taste for seasoning, and serve. Makes 6 servings.

Pork

PORK-APPLE-CABBAGE SKILLET

    4 pork chops about ½-inch thick
    2 tart red-skinned apples
    1 small head white cabbage
    1 cup apple juice
    1 teaspoon caraway seed
    salt and pepper

Brown pork chops in large skillet over medium heat about 3 minutes on each side. Meanwhile, cut apples in eighths and core. Cut cabbage in wedges, then lengthwise in ½-inch slices. Remove chops from skillet. Add apples, cabbage, and apple juice. Put chops on top; sprinkle with caraway seed and salt and pepper to taste. Cover and simmer 20 minutes, or until chops are tender. Makes 4 servings.

PORK FRIED RICE

Try the Oriental way with leftovers. Children love it.

    1 shoulder pork chop (about 6 ounces), cut in 1-inch strips, or 1
        cup shredded leftover pork roast, smoked shoulder, or ham
    soy sauce
    3 tablespoons oil
    1 carrot, finely diced
    3 green onions, cut in ¼-inch pieces
    2 cups cooked rice, chilled
    ½ cup leftover cooked vegetable (peas, green beans, broccoli)
    2 eggs beaten with 1 teaspoon oil

Toss pork with 1 tablespoon soy sauce. Heat oil in wok or large heavy skillet over high heat; add pork and carrot and stir-fry until pork is cooked through or leftover meats are heated. Add onions, rice, and leftover vegetable and stir-fry over medium heat until heated through. Make well in center so bottom of pan is exposed; add eggs and cook, stirring constantly, until softly scrambled, then mix into rice mixture. Stir in 1 tablespoon soy sauce, or to taste. Serve at once. Makes 4 servings.

SCALLOPED POTATOES WITH HAM AU GRATIN

½ cup chopped onion
¼ cup butter or margarine
¼ cup flour
½ teaspoon dry mustard
½ teaspoon salt
⅛ teaspoon pepper
2¼ cups milk
1 cup shredded Cheddar cheese
4 cups thinly sliced pared potatoes
1 pound ham (about 2 cups), cut in chunks

Cook onion in butter in large saucepan until tender. Blend in flour, mustard, salt, and pepper. Gradually stir in milk; cook and stir over medium heat until sauce thickens. Stir in cheese. Arrange potatoes in greased 12 x 8 x 2-inch baking dish. Top with ham and pour sauce over all. Cover with foil and bake in 350° oven 45 minutes. Uncover; bake 15 minutes longer. Let stand 10 minutes before serving. Makes 4 servings.

VARIATION

Cauliflower Casserole
Instead of potatoes, use 1 medium head of cauliflower, broken up into flowerets and parboiled for 10 minutes. If desired, substitute ½ cup of the cooking liquid for some of the milk. Proceed as above.

PORK-WATERCRESS SALAD

The sharp tang of watercress contrasts nicely with the richness of pork.

1 cup mayonnaise
2 tablespoons grated orange peel
¼ cup orange juice
2 tablespoons minced chives
pinch of dried thyme
3 cups diced cooked pork
1 bunch watercress, chopped
1 unpeeled medium apple, diced
lettuce leaves, preferably Boston or Bibb
1 orange, peeled and sliced
1 medium-sized avocado, peeled and sliced

In large bowl, beat well mayonnaise, orange peel, orange juice, chives, and thyme. Add pork, watercress, and apple; toss lightly to coat. Serve on bed of lettuce, garnished with orange and avocado slices. Makes 4 servings.

Lamb

ETLI KEREVIZ

This Turkish lamb and celery root stew is subtly flavored with lemon and thickened with egg. Serve it with pita (flat bread) or an honest French or Italian loaf.

- 1 pound boneless lamb shoulder, cut in 1-inch pieces
- 2 tablespoons oil
- 1 large onion, sliced
- 1 teaspoon salt, or more to taste
- ¼ teaspoon pepper
- 2 pounds celery root, peeled and cut in 1-inch pieces (see note)
- 2 eggs, beaten
- 2 tablespoons lemon juice

Brown lamb in oil in heavy saucepan or Dutch oven. Add onion and cook 5 minutes. Sprinkle with salt and pepper. Add 2 cups water and celery root. Bring to boil, cover, and simmer 1 hour, or until lamb and celery are tender. (If stew gets too thick during cooking, add more water.) Skim. Mix eggs and lemon juice and stir in a small amount of sauce. Stir back into stew. Taste for seasoning and serve at once. Makes 4 servings.

Note: Peel and cut celery root just before adding it to stew to avoid discoloration.

BRAISED BREAST OF LAMB WITH BEANS

2 pounds breast of lamb, cut in serving pieces
1 teaspoon salt, or more to taste
½ teaspoon dried rosemary
1 medium onion, sliced
1 pound green beans, cut, or 1 package (10 ounces) frozen cut green beans
1 cup fresh lima beans, or 1 package (10 ounces) frozen baby limas
12 cherry tomatoes (optional)

Brown lamb pieces slowly in large skillet. Pour off all fat and sprinkle meat with salt, pepper to taste, and rosemary. Add onion, cover, and cook very slowly, adding a little water if necessary, 1½ hours, or until nearly tender. Skim off any fat and add a little water to drippings. Add beans, cover, and cook 20 minutes, or until all is tender. If desired, add a few cherry tomatoes just before serving and heat slightly. Makes 4 servings.

MOUSSAKA

Serve moussaka with tossed green salad with oil and lemon dressing; serve grapes and cookies for dessert.

1 medium eggplant (1 to 1¼ pounds), peeled and cut in ½-inch slices
1 medium onion, chopped
1 pound ground lamb or beef
1 tomato, peeled and chopped
1 can (8 ounces) tomato sauce
1 teaspoon oregano
1 teaspoon salt
1 tablespoon chopped parsley (preferably the flat Italian kind)
white sauce (see recipe below)
¼ cup grated Parmesan or Romano cheese

Broil eggplant slices or fry them in hot oil; set aside. Sauté onion in 1 tablespoon oil until tender, about 5 minutes. Crumble in meat; cook until meat is browned. Pour off excess fat. Stir in tomato, tomato sauce, oregano, salt, and parsley. Cook, stirring occasionally, until sauce is thick and liquid has cooked down. Meanwhile, prepare white sauce. Put half of the eggplant slices in bottom of greased 12 x 8 x 2-inch baking dish, spread meat evenly, then top with rest of eggplant. Spread sauce evenly over top; sprinkle with Parmesan. Bake in 350° oven 30 to 40 minutes, or until bubbly. Makes 6 servings.

White Sauce

Melt 2 tablespoons butter or margarine in saucepan; stir in 2 tablespoons flour. Gradually stir in 1 cup milk and ½ teaspoon salt. Cook, stirring, until thickened. Cool slightly and beat in 1 egg. Makes about 1¼ cups.

7

BREADS, PIES, PUDDINGS, COOKIES, AND CAKES

Vegetables have managed to find a place everywhere on the menu. Faced with a surplus of one vegetable and a shortage of everything else but ingenuity, some gifted cook somewhere, sometime, found a way to use that vegetable, be it for bread or cake or some kind of dessert.

Americans are used to creations like sweet-potato pie and pumpkin chiffon pie, which tend to shock our foreign visitors. Potatoes, however, have been used to make sweets for centuries in central Europe; for instance, in cakes such as almond-potato torte, which appears toward the end of this chapter. For that matter, what are we to make of a sauerkraut-cocoa cake, or crème d' abacate (sweetened avocado cream)?

A few of the recipes in this chapter are relatively complicated or time-consuming, but most of them are not. Two at least are child's play: pumpkin tea loaf and coconut-carrot bread. People who are serious about their vegetables ought to take time out to try some of these offbeat recipes for a quick and pleasant change of pace.

Breads

ZUCCHINI-PARMESAN BREAD

3 cups flour
1 cup shredded zucchini
⅓ cup sugar
3 tablespoons grated Parmesan cheese
5 teaspoons baking powder
½ teaspoon baking soda
1½ teaspoons salt
⅓ cup butter or margarine
1 cup buttermilk (see note)
2 eggs
2 tablespoons grated onion

Mix flour, zucchini, sugar, cheese, baking powder, soda, and salt. Melt butter, stir in buttermilk, eggs, and onion until smooth, then stir into flour mixture just until mixed (mixture may seem dry). Spread in greased 9-inch loaf pan and bake in preheated 350° oven 55 to 60 minutes, or until pick inserted in center comes out clean and loaf pulls away from sides of pan. Cool in pan for 10 minutes, then remove and cool thoroughly on cake rack. Makes about 10 servings.

Note: If you don't have buttermilk, measure 2 tablespoons vinegar into cup and add milk to make 1 cup.

SWEET-POTATO BISCUITS

1½ cups flour, sifted
4 teaspoons baking powder
¾ teaspoon salt
½ cup shortening
¼ cup milk
1¼ cups mashed, cooked sweet potatoes
5 slices crisp bacon, crumbled

Sift dry ingredients; cut in shortening. Combine remaining ingredients and add to first mixture. With fork, mix until soft dough is formed. Roll or pat ½-inch thick on floured board. Cut with floured 2½-inch cutter. Bake in preheated 425° oven, 15 minutes, or until golden. Makes 10 to 12 biscuits.

PUMPKIN-RAISIN ROLLS

1¼ teaspoons salt
½ cup sugar
¼ cup butter or margarine
1 envelope dry yeast
1 cup canned pumpkin
1 cup golden or dark raisins
about 4½ cups all-purpose flour

Put salt, sugar, and butter in large bowl and add 1 cup hot water. Stir until butter is melted. If necessary, cool to lukewarm. Dissolve yeast in ¼ cup warm water and stir into mixture; add pumpkin and raisins. Add half the flour and beat well with wooden spoon. Then stir in enough more flour to make a soft but firm dough. Turn out on floured board and knead 5 minutes, or until dough is elastic. Put in greased bowl and turn greased side up. Cover and let rise in warm place 1 hour, or until doubled in bulk. Punch down and shape in 2-inch balls. Put in greased large muffin-pan sections or arrange side by side in greased baking pan. Let rise 30 minutes, or until doubled in bulk. Bake in preheated 375° oven about 20 minutes. Serve at once. Makes about 2 dozen rolls.

PUMPKIN TEA LOAF

2½ cups all-purpose flour
½ cup wheat germ
3 teaspoons baking powder
1½ teaspoons salt
1 teaspoon baking soda
1 teaspoon cinnamon
½ teaspoon nutmeg
½ teaspoon ginger
¼ teaspoon ground cloves
1½ cups sugar
½ cup vegetable oil
2 eggs
1½ cups canned pumpkin

Stir together the flour, wheat germ, baking powder, salt, baking soda, cinnamon, nutmeg, ginger, and cloves in a bowl or on a piece of waxed paper. Put the sugar, oil, and eggs in a large bowl and beat until creamy. Blend in the pumpkin. Add the dry ingredients and mix only until they are moistened. Spread in a greased 9-inch loaf pan and bake in preheated 350° oven 1 hour, or until a toothpick inserted in center comes out clean. Cool in pan on cake rack for 10 minutes. Remove from pan and cool thoroughly. Wrap and store overnight for easier slicing. Makes about 10 servings.

COCONUT-CARROT BREAD

This is a very sweet loaf that ages exceptionally well. No milk or other liquid is necessary in this recipe.

3 eggs
½ cup vegetable oil
1 teaspoon vanilla extract
2 cups finely shredded carrots (4 or 5 medium carrots)
1 package (7 ounces) flaked coconut
1 cup chopped walnuts
1 cup raisins

2 cups all-purpose flour
1 cup sugar
1 teaspoon each baking powder and soda
1 teaspoon cinnamon
½ teaspoon salt

Beat eggs until light. Stir in oil, vanilla, carrots, coconut, walnuts, and raisins. Mix remaining ingredients and stir into first mixture. Spread in greased 9-inch loaf pan and, to prevent excessive browning, bake on low rack in preheated 350° oven 70 minutes, or until top springs back if lightly pressed and sides shrink away from pan. Let stand on cake rack about 10 minutes, then turn out and turn right side up. Cool thoroughly. Makes about 10 servings.

CORN WAFFLES

1 cup corn pulp or cream-style corn (see note)
2 eggs, beaten
1 teaspoon sugar
½ teaspoon salt
about ¾ cup milk
butter or margarine
2 cups all-purpose flour
3 teaspoons baking powder
maple or other syrup

Mix corn, eggs, sugar, salt, and milk together and add 1 tablespoon melted butter. Sift in flour and baking powder; mix well. Add more milk if mixture is too thick. Bake in waffle iron. Serve with butter and syrup. Makes 4 to 6 servings.

Note: To prepare corn pulp, take a sharp knife and slit down center of each row of kernels on an ear of corn. Push out pulp and juice with dull edge of knife. Allow 6 ears of corn for 1 cup of pulp.

Pies

PUMPKIN CHIFFON PIE

graham cracker crust (see recipe below)
½ cup brown sugar, packed
1 envelope unflavored gelatin
½ teaspoon pumpkin pie spice
¼ teaspoon ground cardamom
¼ teaspoon salt
2 eggs, separated
¼ cup milk
1 can (1 pound) pumpkin
1 cup sour cream
¼ teaspoon grated lemon rind
1½ teaspoons lemon juice
1 cup heavy cream
chopped nuts

Prepare crust and set aside to cool. In heavy saucepan, mix sugar, gelatin, spices, and salt. Stir in egg yolks, milk, and pumpkin. Put over medium heat and cook, stirring, until mixture bubbles. Remove from heat, cool slightly, then add sour cream, lemon rind, and juice. Beat egg whites until stiff but not dry and fold into mixture. Whip cream and fold in. Pour into crust, sprinkle with nuts, and chill several hours, or until firm. Makes 8 servings.

Graham Cracker Crust
Mix 1⅓ cups graham cracker crumbs, ½ teaspoon ginger, and 6 tablespoons butter or margarine, melted. Press firmly into 9-inch pie pan. Bake in preheated 300° oven 10 minutes.

GREEN TOMATO PIE

6 to 8 medium-sized green tomatoes
2 tablespoons lemon juice
1 teaspoon grated lemon rind
½ teaspoon salt
¼ teaspoon cinnamon
¾ cup sugar
2 tablespoons cornstarch
1 tablespoon butter or margarine
pastry for 9-inch double-crusted pie

Wash tomatoes, peel, and slice ⅜-inch thick. Combine with lemon juice, lemon rind, salt, and cinnamon in saucepan and cook 15 minutes, stirring frequently. Mix sugar and cornstarch. Add to tomato mixture and cook until clear, stirring constantly. Add butter and cool slightly. Line 9-inch pie plate with pastry and pour in mixture. Cover with pastry, seal edges, and cut several gashes to allow steam to escape. Bake in preheated 425° oven 40 to 50 minutes. Serve slightly warm or cool. Makes 8 servings.

SWEET-POTATO PIE

2½ pound sweet potatoes
½ cup light brown sugar, packed
¼ cup butter, melted
½ teaspoon nutmeg
¼ teaspoon cinnamon
3 eggs beaten with ¼ cup milk
unbaked 9-inch pie shell
whipped cream
crystallized ginger (optional)
candied citron (optional)

Boil sweet potatoes in jackets until tender; drain, peel, and mash. Measure out 4 cups in large mixing bowl and blend in sugar, butter, nutmeg, and cinnamon. Stir in egg mixture until thoroughly blended; pour into pie shell and bake on lowest rack in preheated 325° oven 40 minutes, or until lightly browned. Cool on wire rack. Garnish with mounds of whipped cream around rim of pie and sliced ginger and citron, if desired. Makes 8 servings.

Note: You may substitute mashed canned sweet potatoes or yams for the fresh ones.

Puddings

PUMPKIN IN A PUMPKIN SHELL

This is a spectacular fall dessert.

4-pound ripe symmetrical pumpkin
butter or margarine
brown sugar
salt
pumpkin pie spice
milk

Wash pumpkin well, dry, and oil skin. Place on rack in shallow pan with a little water added to pan. Bake in 350° oven about 2 hours, or until tender (test by piercing with skewer). Remove from oven and when cool enough to handle, cut off top third crosswise and scoop out seeds. Scoop pulp into bowl, leaving a little pulp attached to bottom of shell to form a substantial case. (Notch or scallop edges, if desired.) Mash pulp and, for each cup, beat in 1 tablespoon butter or margarine, 1 teaspoon brown sugar, ¼ teaspoon salt, and ¼ teaspoon pumpkin pie spice. If mixture seems heavy, add a little milk. Pile into pumpkin shell, wrap in foil, and bake in 325° oven about 1 hour, or until heated through. Remove foil and place pumpkin on serving dish. Makes about 8 servings.

Note: To make ahead, refrigerate pumpkin a few hours or overnight after filling.

SWEET-POTATO PUDDING

2 eggs
1 cup milk
2½ cups peeled and coarsely grated sweet potatoes, loosely packed (about 1 pound; to prevent darkening, grate just before adding to milk mixture)
¾ cup light brown sugar, packed
1 teaspoon each ginger and cinnamon
¼ teaspoon salt
⅓ cup chopped walnuts
whipped cream, lightly sweetened

In bowl, beat eggs with fork until light. Add milk. Stir in sweet potatoes, then sugar, ginger, cinnamon, and salt. Bake in greased round 1½-quart baking dish in preheated 350° oven 30 minutes. Sprinkle walnuts around edge. Bake 30 to 40 minutes longer, or until slightly puffed and knife inserted in center comes out clean. Cool slightly. Spoon out and serve warm with whipped cream. Makes 6 to 8 servings.

ZUCCHINI APPLESAUCE

2 medium zucchini, peeled and diced
2 cooking apples, peeled, cored, and diced
¼ cup sugar
2 whole cloves
½ teaspoon salt
1 tablespoon lemon juice
½ teaspoon cinnamon

In large saucepan, bring to boil zucchini, apples, sugar, cloves, salt, and ½ cup water. Reduce heat, cover, and simmer 20 minutes, stirring occasionally. Remove cover; continue cooking until all liquid has evaporated. Discard cloves. Mash mixture or blend until smooth. Stir in lemon juice and cinnamon. Cover and refrigerate. Makes about 2 cups.

CRÈME D' ABACATE

Avocado cream is a popular dessert south of the border, where this fruit is often sweetened.

2 large, very ripe avocados
lime juice
sugar
milk
lime slices (optional)
crème de cacao (optional)

Peel and pit the avocados and whirl in blender. Add lime juice and sugar to taste and enough milk to make a heavy mayonnaise consistency. Serve chilled in sherbet glasses, garnished with lime slices or a teaspoon of crème de cacao, if desired. Makes 6 servings.

Cookies

PUMPKIN AND CHOCOLATE CHIP COOKIES

1 cup cooked pumpkin
1 cup sugar
½ cup oil
1 egg
2 cups flour
2 teaspoons baking powder
1 teaspoon cinnamon
½ teaspoon salt
1 teaspoon baking soda dissolved in 1 teaspoon milk
1 cup semisweet chocolate pieces
½ cup chopped nuts (optional)
1 teaspoon vanilla

Combine pumpkin, sugar, oil, and egg. Stir together flour, baking powder, cinnamon, and salt; add to pumpkin mixture along with dissolved soda and mix well. Stir in chocolate, nuts, and vanilla. Drop by teaspoonfuls on lightly greased cookie sheet. Bake in preheated 375° oven 10 to 12 minutes. Makes about 5 dozen.

POTATO RINGS

1 cup flour
½ teaspoon baking powder
¾ cup finely grated cooked potato (1 medium)
½ cup butter or margarine, softened
beaten egg or milk
sugar

Combine flour, baking powder, potato, and butter in mixing bowl; knead with hand to form smooth dough. Divide dough in quarters. On lightly floured surface, shape each piece in long rope ⅜ inch in diameter. Line up ropes parallel to one another and cut across in 4-inch pieces. Form each in ring, pinching ends together. Brush with egg, then dip into sugar. Bake on greased cookie sheet in preheated 350° oven about 15 minutes. Top will still be light and bottom light brown. Cool on rack. Makes about 28.

COCONUT-POTATO DROPS

    1 medium potato, peeled
    1 teaspoon butter or margarine
    ½ teaspoon almond extract
    1 pound (4½ cups) confectioners' sugar
    1 package (7 ounces) flaked coconut
    candied cherries
    nuts

In small saucepan, cook potato in water to cover until tender; drain and mash. Measure ½ cup into bowl and stir in butter and almond extract. Gradually stir in sugar (mixture will be thin at first.) Mix until smooth, then stir in coconut. Drop by teaspoonfuls onto waxed paper. Top each with a cut candied cherry or nut. When cold, pack in airtight container. Makes about 45.

Cakes

TOMATO SOUP CAKE WITH
CREAM CHEESE FROSTING

Tomato soup adds flavor and moistness to this up-to-date version of an old-time favorite.

>   2 cups all-purpose flour, sifted
>   1⅓ cups sugar
>   4 teaspoons baking powder
>   1 teaspoon baking soda
>   1½ teaspoons ground allspice
>   1 teaspoon cinnamon
>   ½ teaspoon ground cloves
>   ½ cup solid vegetable shortening
>   1 can (10¾ ounces) condensed tomato soup
>   2 eggs
>   cream cheese frosting (see recipe below)

Sift together flour, sugar, baking powder, baking soda, allspice, cinnamon, and cloves into a large bowl. Add shortening and soup and beat with electric mixer at low to medium speed 2 minutes. (or 300 strokes with spoon), scraping sides and bottom of bowl constantly. Add eggs and ¼ cup water and beat 2 minutes longer, scraping bowl frequently. Pour into two 9-inch layer pans lined on bottom with waxed paper. Bake in preheated 350° oven 25 minutes, or until done. Let stand in pans on cake racks 10 minutes, then turn out, peel off paper, and turn cakes right side up; cool. Spread frosting between layers and on top of cake.

Cream Cheese Frosting

Blend 1 package (3 ounces) cream cheese with 1 tablespoon milk and ½ teaspoon vanilla. Gradually beat in 2½ cups sifted confectioners' sugar.

POTATO-CHOCOLATE CAKE

⅔ cup butter or margarine, softened
2 cups sugar
4 eggs
1 cup hot mashed potatoes
2 squares unsweetened chocolate, melted
2 cups sifted flour
3½ teaspoons baking powder
1 teaspoon cinnamon
½ teaspoon each nutmeg, ground cloves, and mace
½ cup milk
1 cup chopped nuts
chocolate frosting (see recipe below)

Cream butter and sugar until light and fluffy. Add eggs one at a time, beating thoroughly after each. Add potatoes and chocolate and mix well. Stir dry ingredients together and add alternately with milk, beating after each addition until smooth. Stir in nuts. Pour into greased and floured 13 x 9 x 2-inch pan and bake in pre-heated 350° oven 35 minutes, or until pick inserted in center comes out clean. Cool in pan on cake rack. Spread with frosting. Makes 12 servings.

Chocolate Frosting

3 squares unsweetened chocolate
2 tablespoons butter or margarine
4½ cups confectioners' sugar, sifted (about 1 pound)
¾ cup sour cream
¼ teaspoon salt
1 teaspoon vanilla

Melt chocolate and butter. Remove from heat and cool. Mix sugar, sour cream, and salt. Gradually add chocolate mixture and vanilla and beat well. If too soft to spread, chill until of desired consistency.

ALMOND-POTATO TORTE

6 ounces blanched almonds, prepared day ahead and dried
½ pound unpeeled baking potatoes, cooked and chilled (1 large)
8 eggs, separated
1 cup sugar
grated rind and juice of 1 lemon (3 tablespoons juice)
½ teaspoon mace
1 tablespoon rum
2 tablespoons fine dry bread crumbs or grated almonds

Put thoroughly dry almonds in blender. Whirl on low speed a few seconds, then on high a few seconds to grind evenly. Do not grind so fine they become oily and compact. Peel potatoes and grate on medium grater. Beat egg yolks and sugar together until mixture is light, satiny, and the color of cream. Stir in almonds, potato, and flavorings. Blend lightly. Beat egg whites until stiff and fold quickly into first mixture. Butter a 9-inch springform pan and sprinkle with crumbs. Turn batter into pan. Bake in preheated 325° oven 1¼ hours, or until cake shrinks slightly from sides of pan. Remove and cool in pan, overnight if possible. Torte will sink slightly in the middle. Remove springform rim and put torte on serving plate. Cut in small wedges with serrated knife. Makes 12 servings.

ZUCCHINI CAKE

1½ cups flour
1 teaspoon baking powder
1 teaspoon cinnamon
½ teaspoon baking soda

½ teaspoon nutmeg
½ teaspoon ground cloves
¼ teaspoon salt
1¼ cups brown sugar, packed
¾ cup oil
2 eggs
1 teaspoon vanilla
1½ cups shredded zucchini
whipped cream (optional)

Combine flour, baking powder, cinnamon, baking soda, nutmeg, cloves, and salt; set aside. In large bowl, beat together sugar, oil, eggs, vanilla, and zucchini until sugar dissolves. Stir in flour mixture just until well blended. Turn into greased and floured 10-inch fluted tube pan. Bake in preheated 350° oven 45 minutes, or until pick inserted in center comes out clean. Cool in pan 10 minutes. Turn out on rack and cool completely. Serve with whipped cream, if desired. Makes about 16 servings.

BEET CAKE WITH CHOCOLATE CHIPS

2 cups flour
½ teaspoon salt
2 teaspoons baking powder
⅓ cup cocoa
2 eggs
1 cup sugar
½ cup oil
1 cup grated beets, cooked or canned
2 teaspoons grated orange peel
¼ cup orange juice
1 package (6 ounces) semisweet chocolate pieces
confectioners' sugar (optional)

Mix flour, salt, baking powder, and cocoa; set aside. In large bowl of mixer, beat eggs and sugar until fluffy and lemon-colored. Add oil, beets, orange peel, and juice; beat well. Stir in flour mixture just to blend. Stir in chocolate chips. Bake in greased 9 x 9 x 2-inch pan in preheated 350° oven 40 to 45 minutes, or until pick inserted in center comes out clean. Cool in pan about 10 minutes. Invert on rack to cool thoroughly. If desired, sprinkle with confectioners' sugar. Makes 16 squares.

SAUERKRAUT-COCOA CAKE

It sounds bizarre, but it works. Most people guess there's coconut in the cake.

⅔ cup butter or margarine, softened
1½ cups sugar
3 eggs
1 teaspoon vanilla extract
½ cup unsweetened cocoa
2¼ cups all-purpose flour, sifted
1 teaspoon baking powder
1 teaspoon baking soda
¼ teaspoon salt
⅔ cup chopped sauerkraut, rinsed and drained
cocoa whipped cream (see recipe below)

Cream butter with sugar until light and fluffy. Beat in eggs and vanilla. Sift dry ingredients (cocoa, flour, baking powder, baking soda, and salt) together and add alternately with 1 cup water, beating after each addition until smooth. Stir in sauerkraut. Spread in two greased and floured 9-inch square or round cake pans and bake in preheated 350° oven 30 minutes, or until done. Remove from pans and cool on cake racks. Fill and frost with cocoa whipped cream. Makes 12 servings.

Cocoa Whipped Cream
Put 1 cup heavy cream and ½ teaspoon vanilla in bowl. Mix together 2 tablespoons unsweetened cocoa, 2 tablespoons sugar, and dash of salt and add to cream. Mix well and chill 1 hour; whip.

Index